Anti-Authoritarian Curriculum Practice

Anti-Authoritarian Curriculum Practice

Powerful Theories for Teachers

Daniel J. Castner, Jennifer L. Schneider, and James G. Henderson

BLOOMSBURY ACADEMIC
NEW YORK · LONDON · OXFORD · NEW DELHI · SYDNEY

BLOOMSBURY ACADEMIC
Bloomsbury Publishing Inc
1359 Broadway, New York, NY 10018, USA
50 Bedford Square, London, WC1B 3DP, UK
29 Earlsfort Terrace, Dublin 2, Ireland

BLOOMSBURY, BLOOMSBURY ACADEMIC and the Diana logo are trademarks of
Bloomsbury Publishing Plc

First published in the United States of America 2025

Copyright © Daniel J. Castner, Jennifer L. Schneider, James G. Henderson, 2025

Cover design: Dustin Watson
Cover image © iStock/Bobs-images

All rights reserved. No part of this publication may be reproduced or transmitted
in any form or by any means, electronic or mechanical, including photocopying,
recording, or any information storage or retrieval system, without prior
permission in writing from the publishers.

Bloomsbury Publishing Inc does not have any control over, or responsibility for,
any third-party websites referred to or in this book. All internet addresses given
in this book were correct at the time of going to press. The author and publisher
regret any inconvenience caused if addresses have changed or sites have ceased
to exist, but can accept no responsibility for any such changes.

Library of Congress Cataloging-in-Publication Data Available

ISBN: HB: 978-1-5381-9397-6
          PB: 978-1-5381-9398-3
       eBook: 978-1-5381-9399-0
        ePDF: 979-8-7651-5420-5

Typeset by Integra Software Services Pvt. Ltd.
Printed and bound in the United States of America

To find out more about our authors and books visit www.bloomsbury.com
and sign up for our newsletters.

CONTENTS

PREFACE

Anti-Authoritarian Curriculum Practice is a book motivated by three issues. The first issue is the relatively marginalized status of curriculum studies in education schools. Curriculum and pedagogy are essential elements of education. An educational experience cannot exist without a curriculum. Therefore, one might reasonably presume curriculum studies would be one of the most prominent subfields of educational theory and research, but the opposite seems more accurate. It is growing increasingly common for Curriculum and Instruction (C&I) Departments in Schools of Education to be comprised of subject-area specialists. Because many subject-area specialists also consider educational practice's psychological, philosophical, and social foundations, what makes curriculum theorizing distinct is unclear even among well-informed educators. Amid such ambiguity, contributions from curriculum theorists and other generalists studying educational foundations are frequently devalued. As teachers, teacher educators, and educational researchers, we see endless value in past and present curriculum studies. Curriculum studies is an expansive field in which theorists have addressed innumerable dimensions of (mis/non)educative experiences. Yet, when it comes to influencing everyday practices in schools, curriculum theorists have been sidelined for decades. Many theorists have become content critically analyzing curriculum from the sidelines. Meanwhile, having been increasingly subjected to decades of heavy-handed educational reform policies, many teachers have grown accustomed to curricular consumption and implementation roles. Curriculum theorizing, especially practical curriculum theorizing, is only becoming all the more pertinent as it fades away.

The second issue is the proliferation of authoritarian practices related to curricula in the United States (e.g., Michael-Luna and Castner 2023; Michael-Luna and Castner, 202). While anti-authoritarianism is often presumed to be a stridently partisan stance, we intentionally avoid references to the United States' local, state, or federal politics. Instead of denouncing an authoritarian figure or regime, our focus on authoritarian practices attends to a type of action widely carried out in bipartisan educational reform. An authoritarian practice occurs whenever someone exercises power while sabotaging accountability for how their actions affect others. Distal authorities often make ill-conceived curriculum decisions and promise to hold teachers accountable for outcomes. Teachers are constantly dealing with stupid decisions they did not make and are not authorized to overturn. Dealing with authoritarian practices is especially complicated for teachers because we live in a divided world with combative culture wars and polarizing politics. Finding a core set of ideas or values that serve as common points of solidarity is unlikely in contexts with disparate conceptions of reality, ways of knowing, and ethical codes. Therefore, in section two, we introduce the HI-STAR process as a scaffolding to help teachers consider and reconsider basic curriculum concepts as they holistically imagine and engage in professional study and teaching, assess their students, and reflect upon their practice. The HI-STAR process invites teachers to holistically imagine curricular visions of their own and decide how to engage in professional study and teaching activities intelligently and ethically. Anti-authoritarian practices are and must always be personally and contextually determined.

The third issue motivating this book is our appreciation of education as an intergenerational enterprise. Education is a struggle over the values that shape our visions for the future. Public trust in educational institutions is deteriorating. For decades, curriculum theorists have distrusted conservative ideologies dominating educational policy and practice in the United States, while conservative pundits complain that progressive ideologies dominate curricula through teacher unions and university-based teacher preparation programs. Practical curriculum theorizing, a tradition Jim passes along to Dan and Jen (see section 3), provides a treasure trove of useful concepts for teachers trying to overcome the harm caused by the nefarious politicization of education and authoritarian practices. In the HI-STAR process, we hope readers find supportive ideas that nurture the growth of empowering curricular and pedagogical artistry in contexts dominated by ideological and technical control.

1

Introduction

Anti-Authoritarian Curriculum Practice emerges out of a realization that many of the most contentious issues in education are curricular, and thus far curriculum scholars have been either ill-equipped or poorly positioned to address these issues. As curriculum theorists, we have come to the realization that our previous work together, which contributes to the extensive body of literature on democratic education, also fails to respond to the practical problems teachers are currently facing. We have deep concerns about the dire state of both democracy and education in the United States. Still, we also sense that providing readers with yet another perspective text on the virtues of democracy and how schools would operate if they aligned to such ideals would be tiresomely unproductive. Like teachers, we have limited spheres of influence. We do not have the power to transform how our schools and society operate, regardless of how much we wish we did. Nonetheless, we feel an extraordinary sense of responsibility within the boundaries of our sphere of influence as curriculum specialists. We can help teachers adeptly engage curriculum, but first, it is essential to acknowledge the conditions of practice realistically.

There are ample reasons to believe the American democratic experiment is in peril. Political polarization, misinformation and disinformation, institutional corruption, environmental crisis, economic and social inequalities, and the rising power of authoritarian personalities are among the most acknowledged threats to democracy as a way of life in the United States. Meanwhile, the American system of education suffers from similar symptoms. Battles to control curriculum have persisted throughout the history of American schooling (Kliebard 2004), and amid current polarization, the intensity of these struggles is reaching a fevered pitch. In the past several decades, competing interest groups have sought legal remedies at state and federal levels. However, the courts have proven no more equipped than educators or academics in their efforts to resolve ideological disputes and defer curricular judgments to local school boards' governance (Koganzon

2023). In a pluralistic society with democratic aspirations, there are no easy solutions to even the most basic curriculum problems.[1]

We are equally concerned about the status of public schooling in the United States. While public education has long been lauded as a democratizing social force that can supposedly level the playing field for all the nation's people, American schools are not and have never been equitably funded. Children and families in the United States have unequal access to high-quality educational opportunities. Unsurprisingly, the American system of education produces disparate outcomes as well. Politicians' promises to "reform education" and "fix problems" through standardized accountability systems are likely doing more harm than good when it comes to linking democratic values to educational practices. The resulting top-down mandates and prevailing power structures often constrict participatory experiences for teachers and students in schools. Ironically, despite our nation's long-standing democratic constitution, American schools tend to be structured quite hierarchically, reinforcing strict oversight and habituating compliance and submissiveness as elements of educational experiences. Politicians escape answerability for harmful educational reform mandates by asserting their authority and promising to "hold teachers accountable." Given these realities, it is fair to argue that educational institutions in the United States tend to be structured autocratically, and educational reform policies exhibit illiberal and even authoritarian tendencies, which are inconsistent with democratic aspirations and imagination.

This book also emerges out of a deep respect for hardworking teachers. Teaching is an extraordinarily complex, relational endeavor, but in America, teachers and the act of teaching are too often oversimplified or even belittled and demeaned in the minds and conversations of non-teachers. Phrases that float around in public discourse beautifully reflect this lack of awareness and respect for the intellectual, emotional, and moral complexities of being an educator and the labor that goes into teaching. "Teachers have it easy; they get summers off." "Anyone can be a teacher." "Teachers only work from nine to three for five days a week." "Teachers are overpaid." "Teachers are glorified babysitters." "Those who can, do; those who can't, teach." At the same time, in the United States, teachers are micromanaged and accountable for educational outcomes. While school administrators, educational researchers, and teacher educators can support teachers in important ways, teachers' proximity to the children, adolescents, and families of a particular community, as well as their knowledge about the contextualizing situations and conditions unique to their school, are irreplaceable ingredients of sound educational decision-making.

Given the current conditions of democracy, education, and the undemocratic ethos of schools in the United States, engaging curriculum is a tall order. There is an extensive history of curriculum theorists conceptualizing visions for what constitutes a *good* education within a society with democratic aspirations. Thus far, curriculum theorists like us have been ill-equipped to respond to destructive and even authoritarian educational reform policies. We believe theorists' contributions can be helpful, and they indeed influence this book's content. However, we are also aware of the limitations and ambiguities associated with theorists' inclinations to provide teachers with informative theoretical prescriptions and explanations. For teachers, the autocratic structures of schooling are not an abstract problem with a theoretical remedy. Teachers' problems of practice are dynamic and complex. The relational, entangled features of everyday classroom life can never be fully known or predicted. Teaching is a personal, temporal, and contextual form of art, and a teacher's sense of professional beliefs and values are as valid as theorists' more jargon-laced proposals.

As curriculum theorists, therefore, we will not attempt to provide answers from the ivory tower that either prescribe a particular approach to teaching or explain democratic virtues to teachers. Instead, appreciating that engaging curriculum is a practical endeavor, we will introduce curriculum concepts that have empowered us on our journeys as teachers and continue to enrich how we contemplate education and move through educational spaces and places. We do not consider these concepts panaceas or a kind of "best practice" recipe. Nonetheless, we consider them powerful, yet frequently underutilized or overlooked, resources that are potentially useful to conscientious teachers who share our concerns about past and present signs of authoritarianism hindering education in the United States. We frame these resources within a three-part process, which we call HI-STAR.

The following section briefly overviews three philosophical premises underlying our conception of engaging curriculum. Then, we briefly introduce the HI-STAR process. HI-STAR is a recursive inquiry process that uses curricular concepts as *powerful tools* for broadening and deepening teachers' curricular engagements and, in turn, pedagogical practices and students' learning. By conceptualizing a process for contesting authoritarianism and promoting democratic ways of knowing and being through education instead of explaining democratic virtues or prescribing curricular aims and instructional methods, HI-STAR recognizes the potency of empowered teachers' potential for engaging curriculum.

Three Premises of Engaging Curriculum

The HI-STAR process is a framework for engaging curriculum that is based upon three main premises. *The first premise is that teachers are not merely passive recipients of curriculum, and that teaching involves much more than instrumental curriculum implementation.* Teachers make countless decisions related to planning and enacting curriculum every day, and few matters have a more profound impact on what is experienced in schools than the content of the curriculum and how it is mediated in classrooms. A curriculum is much more than content standards prescribed by a state department or the instructional plans and materials provided in a prepackaged program purchased from cooperate vendors, although these are important facets of a curriculum. A more holistic curriculum involves at least three factors: the subject matter, the needs and interests of students, and the societal aims and values. Classroom teachers are optimally positioned for engaging curriculum because day-to-day curriculum is expressed pedagogically. This means the purposes and content of the curriculum are inseparable from how it is enacted and experienced, which leads to our second premise.

The second premise is that teachers are a nexus of power typically understated and underestimated, if not overlooked, in the United States. While teaching is a marginalized profession and seen by some as relatively low status in the United States, what happens in schools impacts an expansive variety of stakeholders. If teachers' work were inconsequential, there would not be such an extensive history of conflicting interest groups trying to control curriculum and teaching (Kliebard 2004), a reality also playing out before us. Teachers have proximity to pedagogical situations that curriculum theorists, teacher educators, school administrators, and other distal authorities do not and in many ways cannot. Therefore, teachers are uniquely positioned to engage curriculum in meaningful ways by exercising sound contextualized judgment, responding to the particularities of people (i.e., students, administrators, families, and communities) and the states of affairs specific to their classrooms and contexts. There are instrumental and moral dimensions to teachers' work, and teachers' actions and leadership efforts with curriculum can vary in effectiveness. Curriculum and types of curriculum leadership, therefore, can exhibit moral qualities attributed to democratic or autocratic ways of life.

The third premise is that engaging curriculum is a form of pedagogical artistry that is continuously created and refined through experience. Pedagogical artistry is unique to each teacher and is the refined, creative expression of their teaching, defined by their growth in awareness, responsiveness, and adaptability. Attempts to overly instrumentalize curriculum engagements on the one hand and overly politicize curriculum on the other impose constraints upon teachers that hinder acts of pedagogical artistry and its growth. There are always instrumental and political dimensions of curriculum and pedagogy, but avoiding reducing educational experiences exclusively to these dimensions is important. Schools are often pressured to engage instrumentalist controls to justify their effectiveness. This is done by documenting measurable outcomes; quantitative data is almost always used as the only valid information. Thus, schools often adopt somewhat prescriptive programs aligned to standardized aims. Teachers' performance evaluations are sometimes contingent upon their adherence to scripted curricula and their students' performance on standardized assessments. At the same time, antagonistic politicians have become accustomed to using education as a political football. Rival political interest groups have competed to control curricula since the beginning of the American system of schools (Kliebard 2004), and "culture war" battles now place unhelpful constraints on teachers. While instrumental and political control are formidable obstacles, many teachers still find and create opportunities to envision, pursue, and practice their pedagogical artistry.

From the American educational philosopher John Dewey (1859–1952) onward, educational theorists have contributed many important conceptual insights about democratic education that resonate with these three premises for engaging curriculum. However, abstract philosophical ideas, even pragmatic ones like Dewey's, often disembody curricular and pedagogical action, and they can be difficult to concretize in the realities of everyday curriculum and pedagogical practices. Not to mention, democratic aims remain aspirational values within American schools and in the greater society. While the United States is one of the world's longest-standing examples of a nation with a democratic constitution, living up to the promises of democracy is a perennial challenge, and there is no guarantee a democratic constitution will survive in this or future generations. On the eve of the Second World War, Dewey ([1939] 1989) reflected on the state of democracy with a sense of uncertainty for its future that is still in many ways relevant today. He wrote that "we have advanced far enough to say that democracy is a way of life. We have yet to realize that it is a way of personal life and one which provides a moral standard for personal conduct" (101). Democracy today is still understood as a political concept, system of governance, and way of life, and it is fair to say that as a collective, we are still living within the tensions of how democracy might become an intrinsic part of how individuals move through the world and relate with others. How might we embody democratic ways of knowing and being as part of our daily lives and within the institutions in which we, as educators, work?

The limitations of past and present attempts to realize democracy as a way of life in school and society restrain the extent to which practical conceptions of democratic curriculum leadership are viable. When experiential realities temper democratic aspirations, it is imperative to acknowledge that democracy as a way of living is still very much in its infancy, and constitutionally expressed ideals often lack corresponding experiential knowledge and skill. Practical utility is an outgrowth of concrete experience. Despite our desire to advance principles of liberal democracy by linking curriculum to democratic ideals, it is fair to say we have few robust and thriving models or concrete examples of democratic living in our everyday lives, relationships, and institutions. In comparison, autocratic and even authoritarian habits that favor obedience and systems for controlling practice are commonly experienced by teachers and students in educational institutions from early years to higher education.

For dedicated educators, engaging curriculum against authoritarianism is a realistic endeavor that we believe can be supported by powerful curriculum theorizing. According to Deng (2018), powerful curriculum theorizing has been in short supply, but it is identified by three key features, which align with our three premises for engaging curriculum. First, powerful curriculum theorizing recognizes the primacy of teaching practice and its artistry. Whereas theoretical perspectives produce generalizations through inductive and deductive methods and reasoning, practical artistry considers the particularities of specific people and contexts for deliberative action. Appreciating that a teacher's practice has wisdom and dignity of its own fosters a recognition that teachers are not merely passive recipients of curriculum, and their experiences and potential contributions extend far beyond the efficient and effective implementation of curricular programs. At the same time, theory can empower practitioners by providing concepts and language alongside provoking questions that help them become more conscientious about seemingly mundane activities. Theory can also help teachers become more conscientious of alternative possibilities and intentional in their curricular decisions; however, powerful curriculum theorizing positions theory and practice in reciprocity rather than hierarchically. Theory does not stand above and inform practice, nor does theory need to be translated into practice. Moreover, theorizing is a human activity; it is a practice. Hence, appreciating the primacy of practice is about recognizing the equality of each stakeholder's experiential understanding as having a dignity and value of its own.

Secondly, powerful curriculum theorizing appreciates the need to understand the inner workings of schools. Curriculum does not begin with a blank canvas, nor does it exist in a vacuum. Rather, it occurs within the structures of existing norms of institutions and policies. Contemporary schools' norms, habits, and customs tend to be built upon fatally flawed foundations of standardization and control (Tienken 2017). Such norms futilely rely upon theory to produce a panacea, but there are no silver-bullet solutions to the looming threats of autocracy in American schools and society. Furthermore, educational stakeholders are not waiting for theorists to provide them with a worldview or answers. Stakeholders bring preexisting beliefs, values, and expectations that are consciously known as well as subconsciously held to curriculum deliberations. As intellectually and morally engaged participants in curriculum practice, teachers' power is typically understated in the United States, if not dismissed outright.

Lastly, eclecticism is a key feature of powerful curriculum theorizing (Deng 2018), integrating diverse insights and practices to respond to and address complex educational challenges. While so-called "best practices" in education that try to universally define "what works" have some practical value, they are of limited utility for pedagogical artistry. Although evidence-based instructional strategies can be useful for acquiring standardized outcomes, they are not conducive to open-ended, creative, and imaginative educational experiences. They are tools that can be quite useful for their intended purpose but poorly designed for other tasks. Pedagogical artistry involves knowing how to use a theoretical toolkit judiciously, selecting the right tool for the job and sometimes improvising to allow for and even nurture outcomes that are not and could not have been predetermined. The openness and spontaneity of pedagogical artistry require theoretical eclecticism to respond to the unknowability and unpredictability of practice. Ethically responsible, empowered pedagogical artistry is developed over time through ongoing and deeply personalized journeys of understanding.

To summarize, this book introduces a three-part process that invites teachers to engage curriculum against authoritarianism. This process, called HI-STAR, recognizes the dignity of practice, the common forces that typically control school operations, and educational stakeholders' diverse bodies of experience. HI-STAR is a recursive inquiry process that frames seven basic yet underutilized curriculum concepts as powerful tools for teachers striving to make educational experiences more democratic and less autocratic.

1. curriculum platforms
2. curriculum orientations
3. approaches to curriculum action
4. curriculum study
5. pedagogical artistry
6. expressive 3S learning outcomes
7. reflective teaching

The relevance of these curriculum concepts permeates multiple levels of curriculum decision-making.

The HI-STAR Process

HI-STAR is an acronym for holistically imagined study, teaching, assessment, and reflection. The HI-STAR process frames powerful curriculum concepts for supporting curriculum engagements and reinforces the three main qualities of powerful curriculum theorizing. First, appreciating the dignity of practice, the process will not provide theoretical solutions to practical problems. Instead, HI-STAR provides a scaffolding that puts theory and practice in dialogue to support practitioners' contextualized problem-solving. Secondly, the HI-STAR process is attentive to the inner workings of schooling. The current conditions of contemporary schooling present significant barriers to democracy as a way of life. Bureaucratic hierarchies and top-down accountability often exhibit attributes more readily associated with autocracy than democracy. Thirdly, HI-STAR embraces theoretical eclecticism. The United States is a pluralistic society claiming aspirations of democratic governance and democracy within individuals' lives. Therefore, representatives of citizens' diverse worldviews, experts' various disciplinary perspectives, and stakeholders' particular bodies of experience must be empowered as equal participants in educational discourse and practice.

The HI-STAR process consists of three main components. It is a recursive cycle encompassing the intended, operationalized, and received curricula that many teachers must navigate. The process begins with intentions by holistically imagining one's personal curriculum platforms in relation to contextualizing circumstances. Next, curriculum is operationalized when teachers take action, addressing varied growth pathways in their own professional study and teaching practices. Then, once curriculum has been enacted and received, the third part of the process involves assessing student outcomes and reflecting upon pedagogical practices. These three components of the HI-STAR process will now be described in greater detail.

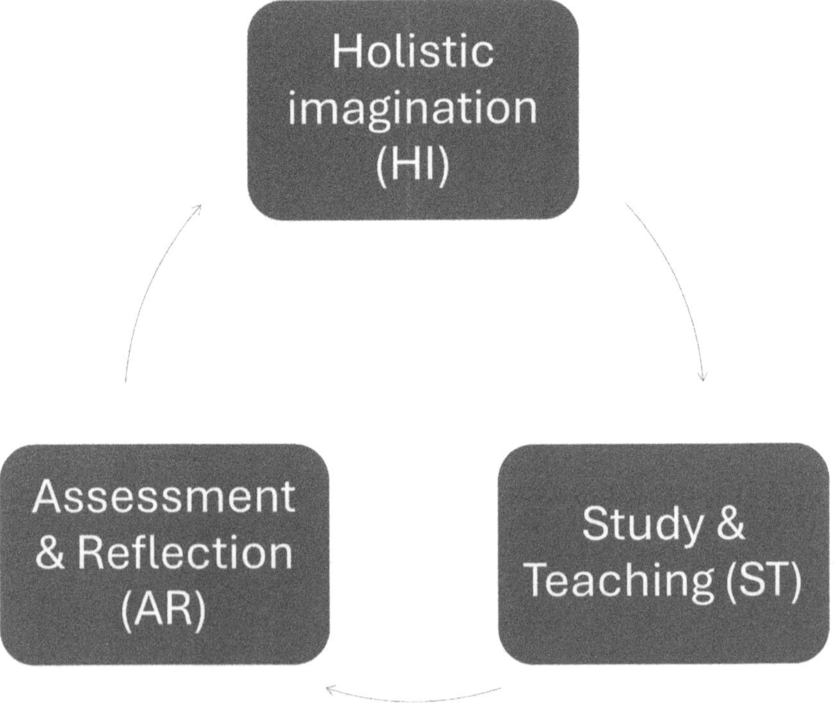

FIGURE 1.1
(SOURCE: AUTHOR)

This diagram depicts the HI-STAR process as a continuous, interconnected cycle of three core components: Holistic Imagination (HI), Study & Teaching (ST), and Assessment & Reflection (AR). Rather than distinct stages, these elements interact dynamically, with each component feeding into and reinforcing the others. This recursive flow allows teachers to continuously examine curriculum purposes, study and teaching practices, and reflective assessments, creating a responsive approach to personal, professional growth toward anti-authoritarian practices.

Holistic Imagination (HI)

The first part of the HI-STAR process is holistic imagination. Three curriculum concepts—curriculum platforms, curriculum orientations, and approaches to curriculum action—are powerful tools for considering a holistic image of the possible ways teachers can engage curriculum. These three concepts are briefly introduced in this section, but further guidance is provided in chapter 3.

To imagine a holistic curriculum platform, teachers bring what they have come to know about education through their lived experiences to their practices. A curriculum platform is "the system of beliefs and values that the curriculum developer brings to his[/her/their] task and that guides the development of the curriculum" (Walker 1971, 52). A holistically imagined curriculum platform lends itself to pedagogical artistry in ways that more narrowly conceived platforms do not. Narrowly conceived platforms often separate curriculum from pedagogy, subordinating teachers to a passive role of merely implementing mandated curricular content that has been preselected for them. Holistically imagined platforms, by contrast, recognize the validity of various and sometimes conflicting "curriculum orientations" (Eisner and Vallance 1974). Mediating and unpacking competing values of conflicting curriculum orientations requires cultivating one's pedagogical artistry as a teacher.

Hence, a holistically imagined platform empowers teachers to be more conscientious about how everyday curriculum decisions are, can, and might be justified. Teachers tacitly or deliberately make numerous consequential decisions when formulating their curriculum platform. When teachers are operating through/with artistry, they are equipped to thoughtfully respond to questions about why subject matter has been selected for an educational experience, how those experiences are deemed advantageous for students' growth, and why the educational experiences are deemed socially valuable. Subject matter is derived from some combination of the content and methods of academic disciplines or "real-world" applications. Students' needs and interests are interpreted with reference to some combination of developmental and learning theories on one hand and in response to students' expressions of needs, interests, and desires on the other. Lastly, curriculum aims to either maintain or transform normative societal values. Transformative aims can aspire toward progressive or regressive social visions.[2] Let us consider an illustration of holistic imagination with Mark, a preservice educator.

Mark aspires to be a high school science teacher. Reflecting on an early field experience, he explained how many of his students do not want to be in his biology class. Mark is a strong student. He has a pleasant, easygoing personality. One day in class, he explained his situation to his classmates: "Science class can be hard. Biology is a graduation requirement, but it is not for everyone! I just try to make the most of it. I tell the kids, 'Hey, this is just something you've got to do, and I am here to help. Let's just work together and get through it.' I think being nice and honest with them goes a long way, and they appreciate it."

Mark's affable demeanor will undoubtedly serve him well as a teacher. However, what he describes is an example of a commonly missed opportunity to engage curriculum. Why is this worth knowing and experiencing is always a valid curriculum question. Instead of justifying the course as merely an unavoidable bureaucratic mandate, Mark has an opportunity to convey a broader purpose of science education to his students. These questions and the outline below can help him consider a more holistic 3S curriculum platform.

- Subject matter: The natural sciences in general and biology in particular are important subjects.
  - How will the student be learning new content and ways of thinking about life?
  - How is the content of the course observable in the real world?
- Self: It is good for students to be in his biology class.
  - Why should every high school student learn about life sciences like biology?
  - Why is biology an interesting and engaging subject area?
- Social: There is social value in the learning that happens in this biology course.
  - How is the course relevant to students' anticipated future?
  - Does the content of the course empower students to advocate for social change?

The above vignette demonstrates how Mark could be encouraged to holistically reimagine his curriculum platform. **A curriculum platform** is the system of beliefs and values brought to curriculum development, revision, and implementation. Platforms guide the processes of curricular practices. A **holistically imagined platform** requires the balanced integration of subject, self, and social (3S) learning. The image below draws upon various **curriculum orientations** to prompt considerations made about these three dimensions of platform.

Developing and sustaining a holistically imagined platform involves manifold considerations. In addition to empowering teachers to be more conscientious of everyday curricular decisions, a holistically imagined platform seeks continuity and interaction among subject matter, societal aims and values, and the needs and interests of students. Holistically imagining a platform is an ongoing process that evolves through interactive experiences. Moreover, teachers' personal platform visions and the platform vision of their professional context (i.e., the beliefs of their collegial team or the norms of their school) are not always congruent. Viewpoint diversity, freedom of thought and expression, and cooperative, communicative interactions are vital characteristics of social democracy and prerequisites for nurturing pedagogical artistry and engaging curriculum. Disagreements and the process of navigating them are part of democratic living. However, when teachers' personal and professional platforms encompass beliefs and values that conflict with the beliefs and values comprising contextualizing platforms, they encounter a significant curriculum challenge. Part of teachers' platform development involves identifying whether they are working within a situation of consensus or conflict and deciding how they should proceed. Negotiating professional collaboration is a complex endeavor but considering at least **five approaches to curriculum action** can support teachers' efforts to enact their platforms in relation to institutional platforms.

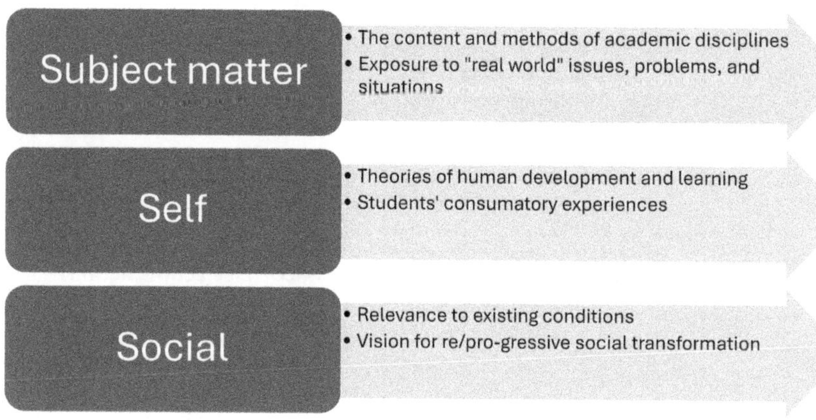

FIGURE 1.2
(SOURCE: AUTHOR)

Table 1.1 juxtaposes five approaches to curriculum action and offers insights for teachers to navigate their platforms in relation to institutional expectations. Each approach is grounded in a specific way including from basis and corresponding actions and practices. These approaches provide a framework for teachers to think through and critically examine institutional platforms as well as help them navigate their own personal beliefs and professional expectations in curriculum work.

In schools operating with basic levels of competency, some practices are worth preserving. In such instances, nonreflective curriculum action is in order. An important part of such curriculum action is knowing what not to change. When curriculum leaders are satisfied with their assessments of outcomes and reflections on corresponding practices, reliance upon past precedent, traditions, and productive habits is justifiable. A common refrain of teachers engaged in **nonreflective curriculum action** might be: "If it is not broken, do not try to fix it." and "This is how we have always done things here, so we keep doing it." Essentially, this approach involves consistently relying upon and implementing what has been done in the past without considering alternative methods or deeply considering other possibilities or potentialities.

The other four types of curriculum action involve more direct forms of problem-solving. When educational stakeholders share common

TABLE 1.1

Approaches to Curriculum Action	Basis	Actions
Nonreflective	Habits and customs	Following past precedent
Technical-managerial	Consensus	Building efficient/effective coherence
Deliberative	Consensus building through collegial conversations	Multi-perspective deliberation
Conflict-oriented	Ethical and political responsibilities	Resistance, opposition, noncompliance
Peace-oriented	Nonviolence, interconnectivity, and interdependence	Noncoercive action, action without force, non-instrumental engagement, transforming inner and outer relationships, civil resistance and disobedience

curriculum aims, curriculum action is sometimes focused on improving efficiency and effectiveness within classrooms and educational institutions. This type of situation invokes **technical-managerial curriculum action**. In such instances, deference to specialized expertise is warranted, and, in summary, curriculum action involves identifying and disseminating the most relevant resources. A commonly expressed sentiment during technical-managerial curriculum action and leadership informed by it might be "We know what we need to do, but we just need to do it better." and "We need to get everyone on the same page with this." However, when stakeholders are not always on the same page about some, if not many, facets of curriculum and pedagogy, oftentimes traditional top-down managerial strategies come into play where decision-making is centralized and involves a chain of command. In other words, power and authority happen in a hierarchy and flow downward through the education setting. Enforcing performance standards, regular evaluations, and rewarding achievements are examples of strategies that used to influence, direct, and even control humans' behavior. Technical-managerial curriculum action can unfold at the national- and state-level but also within a school district, a department, and a teacher's classroom.

When teachers' personal platforms conflict with contextualizing platforms, they often feel pressured to conform to institutional norms and authority figures' expectations. In some cases, teachers might not feel strongly enough about their professional stance to risk the potential struggle of unpleasant professional disputes. Acquiescing to institutional norms and authority is justifiable if the disagreements are inconsequential or about minor issues. Nonetheless, freedom of thought and expression are two key attributes of any curriculum action striving to be democratic. If disagreements are consequential about matters of significance, teachers might find themselves in a situation conducive to **deliberative curriculum action**. In such situations, multiple viewpoints about what our curriculum can and should do coexist. Although perspectives do not align, viewpoints are not interpreted as inherently at odds with one another. The observed differences are acknowledged and embraced. Therefore, productive dialogue and questions are possible and potentially helpful for making educational experiences more democratic. Deliberative conversations among educational stakeholders affected by one's curricular decisions are the ideal and most democratic method for curriculum workers. Considering diverse bodies of experience enables decisions to be made more thoughtfully and carefully. However, deliberation is a time- and labor-intensive process, and due to the number of decisions teachers and school leaders make daily, not all curriculum actions can be or even should be a deliberative activity. Sound judgment is needed to know when to engage in deliberation and when it is more constructive to utilize another method. Other methods are needed where problems are not identified (nonreflective curriculum action) or if there is a readily known answer to a technical problem (technical-managerial curriculum action).

In other situations, the institutional or political structures do not allow for open and productive collegial deliberations. At times, a teacher might argue that institutional norms or authority figures' directives not only do not work but hurt students, particularly students who face systemic marginalization. These cases call for **conflict-oriented curriculum action.** There is an ever-growing abundance of literature highlighting the various ways dominant educational discourses and practices reproduce social inequalities and adversely affect teachers and students who are members of minoritized populations. In addition, schools are usually not democratically structured institutions. When curriculum workers are convinced that educational situations are reproducing inequalities by design and are systematically enforced by bureaucratic management, collegiality and deliberative action might be implausible and unimaginable. In such instances, conflict-oriented curriculum action can involve clandestine classroom practices, organizing and mobilizing a coalition of like-minded stakeholders for activism, as well as overt dissent and political resistance.

Just like some educational contexts and situations do not always enable deliberation for teachers, this might also be a reality with conflict-oriented curriculum action. Teachers might, for example, resist and/or not resonate with notions of forcibly making change or bending systems or individuals to their will, ideas, and ideals. Sometimes, questioning and confrontation might not be possible because of potential consequences and risks a teacher might incur. A far less common but no less important form of curriculum work is **peace-oriented curriculum action.** This form of curriculum action acknowledges that all teachers must work within sets of constraints that they must navigate. This orientation embraces noncoercive action and action without force as necessary when navigating constraints. These do not mean inaction or doing nothing, but instead actions and acting are done in noninstrumental, nonutilitarian ways. There is not a desire to control others and to force upon them particular purposes, means, or ends. There is instead the desire to respect others' autonomy and to not force or manipulate them to act in a particular way. This approach is centered on nonviolence, which goes beyond avoiding physical harm to others and oneself and encompasses compassion toward oneself and others. Cultivating both inward and outer awareness is crucial for personal and societal growth in a peaceful curriculum action. Interconnectedness is also an aspect of this curriculum orientation, as it recognizes the inherent interdependence of all beings, thus promoting unity rather than division. Further qualities such as an openness to differences, embracing uncertainty, harmony, and supporting creative individuality are all essential in this approach.

Study and Teaching Activities (ST)

After teachers holistically consider their personal, contextualized curriculum platforms and the relationship between the two, it is time for action. The second part of the HI-STAR process turns the focus to study and teaching (ST) activities. Within the HI-STAR process, the chief aim of ST activities is to broaden intellectual, moral, social, and emotional horizons. Put simply, the primary purpose of education is to empower students by broadening their horizons, and to do this and to do it well requires teachers who are also actively engaged in the broadening of their own horizons. The two curriculum concepts teachers can use as powerful tools in this part of the HI-STAR process are **curriculum study** and **pedagogical artistry**.

Academic study expands teachers' educational understandings in multifaceted ways, and six forms of curriculum inquiry—practical, personal, critical, dialectical, communicative, and ecological—can contribute to such growth. These forms of curriculum inquiry are different, yet interconnected, pathways that foster human growth, authenticity, freedom, and flourishing for peaceful, socially just, and cooperative ways of life. Study activities of this sort are a lifelong endeavor. However, curriculum study is not the only way teachers' horizons are broadened. Teachers learn not only from their own studies, but also through their experiences actualizing curriculum in their own classrooms. In effect, teachers are simultaneously recipients of what is conveyed in a professional course of study as well as the planners and implementors of curriculum designed for their students.

Hence, when teachers engage curriculum, they have dual responsibilities. First and foremost, they are responsible for fostering students' intellectual, social, emotional, and moral growth by planning and enacting a meaningful course of study that broadens their students' horizons. If curriculum is engaged adeptly, it empowers students. To adeptly engage curriculum in this way, teachers have a secondary responsibility to empower themselves by broadening their own horizons through relevant curriculum studies. Ideally, study and teaching activities should be linked. Either is insufficient without the other. On the one hand, study activities can enliven the imagination of experienced teachers beleaguered by the autocratic tendencies of schools. Without study, curriculum engagements can become confined to the norms of institutional operations. But, on the other hand, the experiential knowledge of a seasoned teacher can ground abstractions from curriculum studies. Curriculum engagements only matter insofar as they are enacted pedagogically, and experiential knowledge is needed to adjudicate which ideas are most relevant, possible, and desirable for enactments of **pedagogical artistry**. Teachers' and students' growth are similar in the sense that they both aim toward the broadening of horizons and oppose systems of social control and indoctrination. Next, we will discuss six forms of academic and professional inquiry and features of pedagogical artistry in greater detail.

Practical inquiry: Problem-solving is emphasized in practical inquiries. It addresses the real-world, everyday challenges specific to a particular state of affairs. Deliberate decisions are pragmatic outcomes rather than prescriptions, descriptions, and explanations. To get started, one might ask questions such as: What issues/problems do I want to better understand/address? What can be improved? What are some of the potential ways I might begin to explore issues/problems? What might be (or are) potential consequences?

Personal inquiry: Introspection, personal choices, individual responsibilities, and the search for authenticity are emphasized in existential inquiries. Subjective experiences, personal perceptions of selfhood, and interconnectedness with others and the world are highlighted, questioning the human condition, identity, and meanings of life. To get started one might ask questions such as: What is my role, purpose, responsibility regarding this issue/problem? Who do I think I am as an educator and human being? How have I come to certain beliefs about education, teaching, students, etcetera? What have my own lived experiences being educated and educating been like?

Critical inquiries: Interrogating established structures of social, cultural, and political power are emphasized in critical inquiries. Shedding light upon taken-for-granted biases and ideological proclivities, critical inquiries strive to identify and contest various manifestations of oppression. To get started one might ask questions such as: What potential inequities are involved? How are concerns related to justice being addressed? How is power operating?

Communicative inquiries: Viewpoint diversity and reciprocal dialogue are emphasized in dialogical inquiry. The interactive co-construction of ideas and values through ongoing conversations is the basis for this form of inquiry. To get started one might ask questions such as: With whom am I (should I be) in dialogue? Who is affected by my curriculum decisions? What are my conversations with others like? What words, phrases, and other discourse are commonly used or not, and why?

Dialectical inquiries: Dialectical inquiry emphasizes exploring contradictions. Its outcomes include understanding how conflicting ideas, values, and beliefs change over time and shape the evolution of prevailing social, political, and cultural perspectives. To get started, one might ask questions such as: What persistent and potentially irresolvable tensions are involved? How often are educational matters discussed (and thought of) regarding either/or dichotomies rather than both/and?

Ecological inquiries: Often, ecology is linked to science through the study of ecosystems and environmental sustainability issues. While this is not wrong, ecological inquiries can also be much broader. Ecological inquiries highlight relationships and connections and how nothing ever exists in a vacuum. Such inquiry explores the interconnectedness and interdependence between individuals, their communities, the environment that shapes educational experiences, and the context in which learning occurs. To get started, one might ask questions such as: How am I nested with/in relationships such as cultural practices and social issues specific to my educational context? How am I participating in these, and how are these inhabiting me?

These six forms of inquiry collectively support curriculum enactments informed by a wide variety of holistic platform images. Controlling or adversarial activities that are competitive, isolating, and/or alienating might provide efficient credentialing procedures. However, these properties indicate a fragmented image of education, which is unlikely to support the broadening of horizons. When connected to a holistic image of pedagogical artistry, study and teaching activities exhibit attributes of creative democracy such as moral-intellectual growth, cooperation, and reciprocal communication. Table 1.2 contrasts study and teaching activities informed by narrow and fragmented platforms with study and teaching activities informed by a holistically imagined platform.

Attending to their students as well as their own intellectual and moral journeys of understanding, teachers express curriculum through enactments of **pedagogical artistry.** When teachers do not engage curriculum holistically, education is narrowed to amoral processes of credentialing and training. The narrow lens of credentialing and training emphasizes the technical efficiency and effectiveness of teaching. Pedagogical artistry requires technical skills as well, but also so much more. Addressing broader platform visions and supported by curriculum studies, a teacher's pedagogical artistry is responsive to the needs and desires of people and situations with multiple and sometimes competing aims that cannot always be anticipated or fully comprehended. Friesen and Su (2003) describe tensions within pedagogical

TABLE 1.2

Credentialing and Training	**Curriculum Study and Pedagogical Artistry**
Instrumental techniques and strategies	Practical inquiry
Standardized achievement	Personal inquiry
Ideological distortion and rigid reasoning	Critical inquiry
Top-down directives	Communicative inquiry
Either/or thinking	Dialectical inquiry
Fragmented organizations and relationships	Ecological inquiry

situations. In part, teaching is the art of deciding when to allow for freedom and when to impose constraints upon one's students, as well as when and how to attend to what is being experienced in the present moment while also attending to preparing students for an anticipated future. In the following vignette, Jen reflects upon a recent experience as a teacher educator. Her reflections illustrate an example of pedagogical artistry.

On the agenda was to continue exploring multicultural issues through touching upon the assigned readings and topics of cultural appreciation and cultural appropriation in teaching art, but as I crossed my classroom's threshold, I was struck by a thick, heavy silence that was punctuated occasionally with a flurry of rapid clicking keyboards and the humming of one row of industrial lighting that had been turned on. Wrinkled foreheads and focused stares were aglow in the blue light of laptop screens. My preservice artists-educators who were spending their weekdays in field placements were usually eating, scrolling on their phones, and chatting before our class began. But that day they seemed to hardly notice one another. They hardly noticed me.

Walking toward my usual spot in the rectangular arrangement of desks I glanced over several of my students' curled postures to see what was affixing their attentions. It was not papers, emails, or social media but the Educational Testing Service's (ETS) Praxis Performance Assessment for Teachers (PPAT). I knew PPAT would be on students' plates but somehow time had gotten away from me, and I became abruptly aware of this pressing reality in my students' worlds. Accreditation and accountability systems and their demands are not unfamiliar to practicing teachers and teacher educators. The teachers-to-be in my classroom, however, were fairly new to navigating such demands and in particular this system that would be determining their futures to teach after years studying, thinking, and practicing artmaking. Years of time and money spent working toward becoming art educators.

As I took in the scene of what the students were living through, the curriculum I planned began to seem less and less important in that moment. Instead, there was a monster taking up space inside the four walls of the classroom. A monster taking up residence in the minds and bodies of the teachers-to-be. A monster professing in its rhetoric and through assigned tasks to have the ability to measure teachers' content knowledge, skills, and readiness to teach effectively in future classrooms. But teaching is anything but certain and is at its most open, humble, transformational, caring, and relational when an educator can make informed decisions in response to what is unfolding in their classroom with students at a given point in time. Issues of art, culture, and diversity needed to wait for another day, another time.

I began class by asking, "How's it going? What's on your minds tonight fellow art educators?" Two of them looked up almost in unison and sighed, "Stressful." And then, the floodgates opened. I cannot recall how many minutes passed filled with students chiming in one after another sharing their feelings and questions around PPAT.

"I don't understand this thing. It doesn't make any sense."

"The same questions are just repeating all the time. Why?"

"We don't talk about teaching art this way with my mentor teacher."

"What's the purpose of doing this, just to check a box?"

"It seems like they don't know anything about making art or teaching it."

From their shares and exhaustion, pre-assessment rose as a topic and was clearly an area of frustration, and so, I turned it into the evening's anchor point. Pre-assessment became a way to try to point out and address the monster to the students in my class while also guiding them to feed it without getting too deeply sucked into its belly and its instrumentalist demands.

With a mostly working blue dry erase marker in hand, I wrote "Pre-assessment" on the board and underneath the question, "What might you want to know from students before you teach your lesson?" Given the small class size, each student had an opportunity to describe a lesson they were envisioning and together we spent the evening brainstorming possibilities for how they each might go about doing quick pre-assessments before their lessons. Peppered into the conversation were observations on ways in which technical rationality, instrumentalism, and scientism are pervasive in curriculum, teaching, and learning. Reflections were also made around imagination, creativity, expression, and unpredictability within artmaking and teaching it. We also explored how such qualities did not seem to fit well and were not welcomed within the certainty and structure demanded by the monster.

Assessment and Reflection (AR)

Assessment and reflection (AR) constitute the third component of the HI-STAR process. Assessing students' educational outcomes and reflective teaching are two topics for which extant literature is abundant. However, as part of the third part of the HI-STAR process, assessment and reflection will be informed by two powerful curriculum concepts: the **assessment of expressive outcomes of students' 3S understanding** and **reflective teaching concerning three levels of curriculum decision-making**. Common discourses of standardization and accountability are insufficient bases for assessment and reflection when educators holistically imagine (HI) curriculum platforms while also engaging in curriculum studies and approaching teaching as pedagogical artistry (ST). As part of the HI-STAR process, approaches to assessment and reflection recognize the absurdity of using standardized assessments to exclusively hold teachers and principals accountable for student outcomes.

Assessment of expressive outcomes of students' 3S understanding accounts for a holistically imagined platform. Returning to Mark's example, a more expansive approach to assessment will be needed as he broadens his platform. Instead of tracking students' success exclusively in terms of passing grades or scores on advanced placement exams, his assessment of student learning would reflect broader aims of fostering human growth, authenticity, freedom and flourishing for peaceful and cooperative ways of life. Of course, these outcomes cannot be standardized, predetermined, or fully controlled. Nonetheless, within the HI-STAR process, Mark would be encouraged to consider his students' expressions of 3S understanding in relation to their understanding of the subject matter, themselves, and society.

Reflective teaching is the second part of this stage of the HI-STAR process. Reflecting upon teaching practices is a matter of great consequence simply because of the commonsensical importance of teachers' everyday decisions. However, appreciating common inner workings as well as the socio-political situatedness of schools is part of appraising pedagogical artistry and its outcomes. Professional educators, including teachers as well as school leaders, work within the parameters of institutional and political norms. Therefore, it is important for teachers to reflect upon their pedagogical artistry not only in relation to their study experiences but also in relation to three levels of curriculum decision-making.

This type of reflection helps teachers consider the breadth as well as the scope of their pedagogical influence. One level of curriculum decision-making is that teachers usually have more control over decisions made in their classrooms than on institutional-level governance. Another level of action around curriculum is generally for school leaders, who typically focus on institutional-level decisions, recognizing that they rely on teachers to facilitate the operations of individual classrooms. In large measure, teachers, school leaders, and other professional educators tend to have only marginalized voices at the state and federal levels where educational policy decisions are made.

Identifying these three levels of curriculum decision-making implies a hierarchical order while at the same time honoring the relative autonomy of practice. Hierarchies of power are commonly part of the reality of educators' professional experiences. Nonetheless, teachers and school leaders often have much broader and more meaningful educational visions. For example, pressures to "teach to the test" are policymakers' imposition on curriculum, teaching, and educational leadership. The onus should be on policymakers rather than teachers to justify curricular decisions made in public policy arenas. Even when they attend to the obligations of so-called accountability-based policies,[3] many professional educators are simultaneously minding more holistic images of education by creating and maintaining meaningful educational experiences that exceed the vocabulary of accountability-based standardization. Moreover, many dedicated professionals appreciate the importance of their decisions, which can influence classrooms, schools, and even the educational profession.

Returning to Jen's example of pedagogical artistry, she conscientiously assessed her students' 3S understanding as best as she could through what students shared with her that evening while also reflecting upon her own platform situations. Her reflections were broadened by ongoing curriculum study that included the six inquiries. She considered:

- *Practically*, what remaining and/or new issues/problems are observable?
- *Personally*, how does the teacher perceive consistencies or shifts in their professional roles, commitments, and responsibilities?
- From the standpoint of *criticality*, what inequities still need to be addressed?
- From a *dialectical* perspective, what remaining tensions need to be negotiated?
- In terms of *communication*, whose perspectives should be (re)considered?
- And *ecologically*, how was the community of learners interconnected and interdependent with various elements of their educational experiences?

Meanwhile, she carefully considered her pedagogical artistry in relation to the various levels of curriculum decision-making. The imposition of the PPAT was a macro-level decision for teacher certification, which Jen had little ability, if any, to control or change. She could have decided to proceed that evening with the well-organized plans she had in mind. However, she recognized how the PPAT impacted how her students were experiencing their teacher preparation program, which included her course. She was also able to tune into the emotional state of students and make a judgment call on what would be the best use of their limited time together that evening. Because she did have direct control over micro-level curriculum decisions in her course, Jen was able to meaningfully respond to macro-level decisions that she found objectionable. It is important to remember that HI-STAR is a recursive process. Therefore, Mark's assessment and Jen's reflection are not concluding steps but rather part of ongoing, ceaseless processes for their educational growth, and their importance was as small sites where curriculum could be engaged against authoritarianism. Assessing students' expressive 3S outcomes and teachers' pedagogical reflections leads us back to the beginning, to holistically imagining curricular possibilities.

Conclusion

In conclusion, engaging curriculum against authoritarianism is a challenging endeavor. Institutional and political influences often interfere with democratic educational practices and democratic ways of knowing, being, and living. Nonetheless, it is worthwhile for educators to continue navigating and persevering despite significant challenges because we play a crucial role in supporting future generations' expanding consciousness and a more democratic society that is yet to be. The HI-STAR process is potentially helpful for supporting educators to cultivate their own educational growth and that of their students. In Dewey's words, linking education and democracy is an ongoing endeavor to "use the good attained for the discovery and establishment of something better."(Dewey [1929] 2007, 84) We hope that the HI-STAR process can aid the discovery and establishment of more democratic schools and, perhaps eventually, more democratic societies.

SECTION ONE

Foundations of Curriculum Practice

Curriculum is more than a set of plans or materials—it's a complex, dynamic space where ideas, values, and societal forces converge. The next two chapters lay the foundation for understanding this multidimensional practice. Chapter 2 introduces foundational curricular concepts and highlights how curriculum theorists have inspired practitioners to think deeply and creatively about their role in curriculum work. Building on this, chapter 3 examines the challenging realities of contemporary curriculum practice, contrasting democratic ideals with the pressures of authoritarian control while proposing anti-authoritarian practices as a path forward. Together, these chapters invite readers to explore curriculum not only as a structured pathway for learning but as a meaningful site for fostering autonomy, critical reflection, and creativity in the face of evolving educational challenges.

2

Engaging in Curriculum Work

To some extent, everyone knows what curriculum is and can give a general description of it. In everyday conversations, curriculum is typically a word that refers to what is taught to students. When discussing curriculum, people often refer to courses, syllabi, lesson plans, or instructional materials in prepackaged commercially produced programs or local curriculum committees. What about you? If you were to define what curriculum is, what might you say? How do you feel when you hear the word *curriculum*? Can you describe why you feel that way? What do you and your colleagues discuss when you engage in curricular conversations? Syllabi, lesson plans, and instructional materials are part of what we invite readers of this book to consider. However, a brief introduction to some key concepts from the curriculum studies literature reveals that there is much more to the curriculum work that matters the most to you.

The literature provides numerous definitions of *curriculum*. Nonetheless, it is common for participants in curricular conversations and even heated debates about curriculum to presume they have a shared understanding of what curriculum is. Nevertheless, despite this assumption, uniformity in understanding can remain elusive. When defined in concrete and instrumental terms, on the one hand, the meaning of curricula can be straightforward in practice. For instance, you can hand a teacher a set of instructional plans or materials for a course, and they then use that in their classroom to teach subject matter. We can then engage in dialogue about instrumental matters such as the quality of these plans and materials. Are these curricular plans and materials likely to deliver their intended goals? How are the materials organized, and to what degree is that in an appropriate sequence? Are teachers expected to adhere to the plans and use the materials, or may they use their professional discretion? These are some examples of instrumental curricular questions.

On the other hand, when defined more broadly, the meaning of curriculum can become quite abstract. Though sometimes complicated and intellectually demanding, these more abstract conceptions of curricula also have important practical implications. When it comes to curricular discourse, sometimes there is more than immediately meets the eye. If we are handed a set of instructional plans or materials for a course, we receive propositions for what will and will not be included and emphasized during instruction. Sometimes, what is omitted or de-emphasized is as important, if not more important, than what is included or emphasized. This is often called the null curriculum. We might then engage in collegial dialogue about who benefits from the status quo of our curriculum while also considering who is potentially marginalized (i.e., dimensions of hidden or implicit curricula). Whose curricular proposals are shaping the status quo of curricular discourse? Whose are not? How can practitioners be more than passive recipients of curricular proposals and demonstrate professional agency? These are far more complex curricular questions to explore and answer.

This book is informed by a broad yet practical conception of curriculum. When we refer to a curriculum, it is important to be clear about what we mean. Defining curriculum in broad yet practical terms is not a new idea. Joseph Schwab (1983, 240) offered a one-sentence definition: "Curriculum is what is successfully conveyed to differing degrees to different students, by committed teachers using appropriate materials and actions, of legitimated bodies of knowledge, skill, taste, and propensity to act and react, which are chosen for instruction after serious reflection and communal decision by representatives of those involved in the teaching of a specified group of students who are known to the decision makers."

With this long sentence, Schwab highlights several key attributes of any curriculum. First, a curriculum is about communication. It intends to convey an educative message, and as with any communicative action, a curriculum often means different things to different people. Second, Schwab recognizes that curriculum development and design are creative processes involving individuals, presumably dedicated teachers, value judgments and authority about what constitutes appropriate materials and actions, and "legitimate bodies of knowledge, skill, taste, and propensity to act and react." Schwab appreciated the value of considering the multiple perspectives of diverse stakeholders. Thirdly, curriculum is fundamentally a practical matter because the materials and actions of a curriculum only matter in how they are used. Hence, teachers are central to curricular decision-making because they know the people for whom the curriculum is designed. Curriculum decisions are made through careful and inclusive deliberative processes in optimal conditions.

Decker Walker (2003, 4) later defined curriculum similarly, albeit more succinctly. He suggests, "A curriculum is a particular way of ordering content and purposes for teaching and learning in schools." Walker focuses on three key facets of curriculum decision-making: content, purpose, and organization. Put differently, Walker conceives of curriculum as a gestalt of decisions related to the ordering of topics, themes, and concepts of a selection of subject areas, chosen for various reasons. Following Schwab and Walker, we appreciate that all these facets of a curriculum and the dynamics of curriculum construction are, in fact, decisions people make. The main goal of this chapter, therefore, is threefold: (1) to help readers notice the nature and key elements of curricula with which they work, (2) to describe the processes of curriculum construction, and (3) to realize that these are decisions that could be made otherwise.

We build upon these broad yet practical conceptions of curriculum and elaborate upon them in two ways. We conceive of a curriculum as representations and presentations of the natural and cultural world in an educational situation. According to Hannah Arendt, education is the gradual introduction of students to the ever-changing world. Engaging in curriculum work calls on individuals to act as, in Arendt's (2006, 186) words, "Representatives of a world for which they must assume responsibility although they themselves did not make it, and even though they may, secretly or openly, wish it were other than it is." Assuming this responsibility involves selecting, creating, and using trustworthy representations of nature and culture to present them to students meaningfully. Natural and human sciences constitute distinct ways of knowing. Therefore, empirical observations are typically represented and presented differently in a curriculum than interpretations of the human condition. Nevertheless, responsible curriculum work points to the world's interconnected natural and cultural elements with integrity and sensitivity.

Making decisions related to curricular content is inseparable from considering the purposes of education. As we consider what and how we teach, it is important also to deeply consider "why questions" to clarify the reasoning and potential alternatives for these decisions. Curricular purposes define the various and sometimes competing bases of knowledge, belief, and value that orient curriculum practices. Put differently, what we teach and how we teach are informed by personal and collective visions that inspire and inform the goals and directions of educational practices. Being mindful of curriculum orientations is crucial when engaging in curriculum practices.

In 1974, Elliot Eisner and Elizabeth Vallance identified five general curriculum orientations. The relevance of these orientations continues to endure fifty years later. More recently, Pamela Bolotin Joseph (2021; 2011) conceived of eight "cultures of curriculum" that she helpfully organized into three main categories. According to Joseph (2011), curriculum leadership tends to work toward individual development, cultural transmission, social transformation, or some combination of these aims. With reference to these three aims, let's consider how notions of curriculum orientations and cultures of curriculum are overlapping and distinctive.

Individual development is fostered through curriculum orientations that emphasize students' development of general cognition and pursuits of self-actualization. Joseph (2022) identified constructing understanding and developing self and spirit as two similar cultures of curriculum. Culture is transmitted through curriculum orientations emphasizing academic rationalism via interdisciplinary study and orientations focused on socially relevant curricular content. Similarly, cultures of curriculum that emphasize connecting to the canon or sustaining indigenous traditions transmit culture. Eisner and Vallance (1974) also acknowledge social reconstruction as a transformative curriculum orientation, while Joseph identifies cultures of curriculum that confront a dominant order or envision peace as socially transformative. Lastly, conceiving of curriculum as a technology is an orientation that emphasizes finding efficient and effective means to uncritically accepted educational ends. Although conceiving of curriculum as a technology is pervasive, and practical efficiency and effectiveness are commonly valued in schools, this curriculum orientation overlooks the moral dimensions (and responsibilities) of curriculum practice.

Although many people may participate in curriculum construction in multiple arenas, Walker (2003) insists that curriculum practices only matter insofar as curricular changes are enacted in classrooms. Curriculum practice involves the creation of tangible curricular materials and the implicit and explicit design of materials-in-use. In this sense, Walker had a very pragmatic perspective on curriculum. Complementing Deng's notion of powerful curriculum theorizing, he suggested that high-quality curriculum theorizing has four main characteristics: validity, theoretical power, serviceability, and morality. The validity of a curriculum theory is expressed through its meaningfulness, logical consistency, and accuracy. Powerful curriculum theories "enable us to act effectively in a wide range of situations because they give us insight about the likely consequences of acting in certain ways or the values, we will uphold by acting, or both" (Walker 2003, 74). Serviceable curriculum theorizing addresses the problems faced in the real conditions of practice, and Walker further reminds us: "Professionals take risks when they choose among moral codes accepted by different groups of clients, but it is always appropriate for a professional to clarify the values used in any particular theory and show how these fare when judged by some appropriate moral standards" (75).

In short, curriculum theorizing is valid, powerful, serviceable, and moral when it clearly explains: (a) the realities of the conditions of curriculum practice, (b) the curricular problems that need to be addressed, (c) the most effective ways of proceeding in an educational situation, and (d) the ethical implications of our actions. In practice, professional educators rarely act alone, and their professional autonomy is often compromised by state-level (and even federal-level) educational reform policies and top-down instructional management at the school level. In this chapter, we highlight many ways professional educators commonly engage in curriculum work. Because curriculum work (and teaching) inevitably involves the exercise of authority, teachers and school leaders need to use their professional authority judiciously and avoid participating in potentially harmful authoritarian practices.

Authoritarian practices are instances where an individual or entity sabotages accountability for the ways they use authority to exert control over others. Avoiding authoritarian practices means accepting the onus for justifying the authority one exercises. Authoritarian practices are prevalent in policies that hold teachers and school leaders exclusively accountable for educational outcomes as if decisions made in public policy arenas have no effect. Though teachers and school leaders are often victims of authoritarian practices, they can also perpetuate them if they are not careful. Whether due to their own experience of strict oversight or a preference for it, school leaders may, in turn, have tendencies to micromanage teachers. The pressures of standardized instructional management often lead teachers to impose strict control over students. In the interest of disrupting authoritarian practices from being passed down through institutional hierarchies, we ask you to consider the arenas, participants, and paradigms involved in curricular problem-solving.

Generally speaking, practical curriculum problems are addressed in at least three arenas (Walker 2003) by at least five decision-makers (Schwab 2013) and according to three problem-solving paradigms (Henderson and Gornik 2007). These curricular concepts prompt three considerations. First, is your professional authority situated in a classroom, local school, district-level committees, or within a broader public policy arena? Secondly, what bodies of experience are participating in curricular deliberations? Schwab (2013) argued that thorough curriculum deliberations require input from five sources that he called curricular commonplaces: subject matter experts, learners, teachers, representatives knowledgeable of the milieu, and curriculum development specialists. The third consideration is related to paradigms of curriculum problem-solving. A curriculum paradigm defines the organizing problem and problem-solving procedures utilized in curriculum practice. While the standardized instructional management paradigm focuses on improving test scores, the constructivist best practice paradigm emphasizes the understanding of subject matter (Henderson and Gornik 2007). These two paradigms can be controlled in a top-down fashion, and they are susceptible to authoritarian practices. However, the curriculum wisdom paradigm positions professional educators as lead professionals with evolving aims related to democratic ways of living (Castner, Schneider, and Henderson 2020). Hence, a love of wisdom paradigm is open-ended and inherently anti-authoritarian.

Next, we will take a brief look at the history of curriculum development in the United States, detailing key figures, educational philosophies, and the evolving aims of curriculum design. We will share examples of how curricula in early US schools were controlled hierarchically, primarily through textbooks that reflected societal norms and values of the time, such as nationalism, religion, and discipline.

A Brief History of Curriculum Work in the United States

It is not uncommon for even experienced educators to think and talk about their curriculum as something they passively receive. In the United States, schools are often hierarchically controlled. Policymakers govern many facets of school leaders' and teachers' discourse and practices. The system of American schools developed between 1830 and the American Civil War (1861–1865), and textbooks were the primary mechanism of curricular control. Noah Webster (1758–1843) was among the most influential educators of the day. He produced texts called spellers, such as *The American Spelling Book* (1831), which were subsequently replaced by mass-produced texts called readers. Walker distinguishes texts that were spellers that "presented the alphabet and a list of syllables to be memorized followed by lists of words and eventually sentences" (2003, 25) from readers, which were texts that "taught children to sound out words presented in meaningful sentences" (28). In both cases, "religion, nationalism, moral virtue, and strict discipline permeated the lessons" (25).

After the Civil War, visions for curriculum reform broadened. Many prominent educational reformers were educated at European universities and were often inspired by trends in education they observed on the other side of the Atlantic. Two very different features of European schooling became quite significant in the evolution of the American school curriculum. The first feature emphasized academic content. William T. Harris (1835–1909), the US commissioner of education at the turn of the twentieth century, was a key proponent of subject-centered curricula. He viewed academic disciplines as the window to the human soul and was a champion for a traditional liberal arts curriculum. The second feature brought a greater focus to what students were experiencing. European theories of education developed by Jean Jacque Rousseau (1712–1778), Johann Pestalozzi (1746–1827), and Friedrich Froebel (1782–1852) suggested that curricula can be led by the needs and interests of children rather than strict adult control. These child-centered perspectives have been especially influential in early childhood education and among progressive educators.

By the late nineteenth century, the National Education Association began assembling curriculum reform committees to set standards for secondary education in the United States. In 1982, Harvard president Charles Eliot chaired the Committee of Ten. The committee developed what would become a lasting template for US high schools' four-year secondary education curriculum. The committee sought to balance competing demands for a core academic curriculum required of all students and specialized courses of study for individual students' diverse talents and interests. Further, the Committee of Ten and the subsequent Committee of Five, which focused on implementing the first committee's recommendations, also commendably attended to considerations of students, teachers, subject matter, and society.

At the origins of curriculum studies, prominent curriculum development specialists, referred to in the literature as administrative progressives, obscured the conflicting values underlying curriculum rather than explaining, clarifying, and working out their consequences. The administrative progressives of the first half of the twentieth century worked within the context of the burgeoning educational sciences. Therefore, Franklin Bobbitt, who is often recognized as the author of the first seminal textbook on curriculum, conceptualized a method for prescribing educational objectives. During a time of rapid industrialization, which led to dramatic societal and economic changes, Bobbitt was responding to curricular problems germane to a system of public schooling that was growing precipitously. The era of industrialization emphasized practices like efficiency, clear structures and steps, standardization, and productivity, and these values permeated education and still do. Curriculum (and even teaching) began to focus on uniformity, standardization, and structured routines, aiming to produce a disciplined, dependable workforce for students' eventual roles in an industrial society.

Viewing school as a social institution that prepares young people for adult citizenship, Bobbitt's (1918) approach to curriculum development involved three steps. The first step was to utilize a method called "task analysis," a survey of adults deemed "well-trained." Task analysis was intended to identify the domains of life one needs to develop to be a "useful" member of society. Bobbitt identified activities related to language, health, citizenship, general socialization, leisure, religion, and parenting as well as mental fitness and finding one's vocational calling as the domains of life that should be emphasized in a curriculum. Secondly, Bobbitt created an extensive list of learning objectives exhibiting an individual's proficiency in each domain. Thirdly, Bobbitt arranged the objectives into a systematic plan to optimize the efficiency of the curriculum he was developing.

Of course, Bobbitt's allegedly scientific approach to curriculum development was not objective and did not achieve any sense of ethical and political neutrality. Determining what constitutes a "well-trained" person and what it means to be "useful" in society are value-laden enterprises. How and by whom these terms are defined are inherently political endeavors. This is because considerations of what is most worth knowing and experiencing in school, which is perhaps the most basic curriculum question, ultimately rely upon a vision of the good life. In many ways, Bobbitt's vision for preparing students for adult life in the early decades of the twentieth century is like contemporary aims of college and career readiness and those for twenty-first-century skills. Both analyze the world as it is in an attempt to prepare students for a world that will inevitably change by the time they begin their adult life. In this sense, these curricular visions reproduce culture and expect "successful" students to accept and adapt to an established order.

Bobbitt's successor at the University of Chicago, Ralph Tyler, recognized that philosophy rather than hard-nosed empiricism was a more appropriate basis for addressing questions about what knowledge is of most worth. The foundation of what is often called "Tyler's rationale" for curriculum development, which remains the modus operandi of most contemporary curriculum practices, is a clearly articulated philosophical screen. According to Tyler (1949), what constitutes valid knowledge, the needs and interests of students, and societal aims and values worth pursuing through education are screened through a philosophy of education. In other words, a coherent set of philosophical assumptions provides a basis for consistently interpreting subject matter, students, and society, which Tyler identified as the three main sources for determining educational objectives. A philosophical position is not overtly suggested in *Basic Principles of Curriculum and Instruction*, Tyler's (1949) short yet incredibly influential text on curriculum development. This is perhaps both the greatest strength and the most significant limitation of Tyler's rationale for curriculum development.

Questions to Ask Yourself About Conventions of Curriculum Development

Questions Inspired by Bobbitt and Tyler

Bobbitt: What do you want your students to be able to know, understand, and be able to do? What domains of life should inform a curriculum?

Tyler: What psycho-philosophic interpretations of knowledge, needs and interests of students, and societal aims and values define the general aims of the curriculum? What learning experiences are likely to accomplish the intended curricular aims? How can these learning experiences be most efficiently and effectively organized? To what extent have curricular purposes been achieved?

Why Is Tyler's Rationale Insufficient?

In the early 1970s, many curriculum scholars began acknowledging that the relationship between curriculum theory and curriculum practice was changing. In Bobbitt's and Tyler's era, curriculum development specialists exercised substantial authority. Bobbitt prescribed educational objectives for schools in major cities, such as Cleveland, Ohio, and Los Angeles, California, in 1915 and 1922, respectively. Tyler was even more influential as an advisor to the administrations of three presidents of the United States (Hlebowitsh 2021). Like Bobbitt, Tyler understood that teachers' primary role is to implement normative curricular aims. However, unlike Bobbitt, he did not prescribe specific educational objectives for schools. Rather, Tyler's rationale for curriculum development framed the process of determining educational objectives within extraordinarily broad psycho-philosophic limits. In a generous light, Tyler can be viewed as an open-minded proponent of viewpoint diversity. From a more critical vantage point, his rationale for curriculum development is ethically and politically vacuous, adhering to the preferences of the prevailing social order.

Tyler's rationale for curriculum development was more nuanced than Bobbitt's. Nonetheless, Tyler's colleague Joseph J. Schwab (1970) provocatively declared curriculum theorizing moribund because it had become overly reliant upon theory. This will seem like an odd assertion to many readers, a curriculum theorist denouncing reliance on theory. What in the world did Schwab mean? By overreliance on theory, Schwab meant theorizing of a certain kind that positions theory above practice. Too often, according to Schwab, curriculum specialists begin with a state of mind or a general theory of education to deduce a set of normative standards to be explained for teachers' implementation. While habitually positioning theory over practice can, in some instances, produce helpful guidelines, Schwab (1970) proposed an alternative practical language for curriculum.

Following Schwab, we strive for this book to be what our friend Thomas Kelly calls a profoundly practical contribution to teachers. A practical language shifts focus to the particularities of a state of affairs to deliberate among various possible courses of action. There is no universally shared theory of education to guide curriculum-making. Therefore, Schwab proposed deliberation conversations among curriculum stakeholders (i.e., subject area experts, teachers, students, milieu, and curriculum specialists) were the best way to make practical curriculum decisions. This doesn't mean that each contributor to the curriculum should have an equal say on every issue. Rather, according to Schwab, each perspective represents a distinct "sphere of experience" that should be accounted for when creating/revising curricula. Schwab built upon the strengths of Tyler's contributions by prioritizing multi-perspective dialogue in curriculum practice.

Similarly, Decker Walker (1971) argued that curriculum can be (and is) developed with various platforms, deliberative processes, and designs. Whether implicit or overtly expressed, these are three necessary elements of any curriculum. First, a curriculum always circulates a platform, a series of beliefs and images about what should be valued/prioritized and what should not. One's curriculum platform can be open-minded, ideologically strident, analytical, impassioned, moderate, extreme, or anywhere in between. Second, curricula are constructed through a process. Walker referenced Schwab's deliberative artistry when writing about the deliberative ideal for careful decision-making. However, he also recognized that deliberative conversations can be time-consuming and inefficient. In practical situations, educators make countless decisions day in and day out. Therefore, it is important to determine what issues warrant careful deliberations and what decisions can/should be made using precedent, habit, or even top-down mandates. Third, numerous decisions that could have been made otherwise constitute the design of a curriculum. When a curriculum is designed differently, it functions differently. For Walker, the purpose of curriculum theorizing is "to make ideals explicit, clarify them, work out their consequences for curriculum practice, compare them to other ideals, and justify or criticize them" (2003, 60).

Questions to Ask Yourself About Deliberative Curriculum Practice

Questions Inspired by Schwab and Walker

Schwab: Among the known alternatives, what are the best courses
   of action for a particular group of people and a specific
   educational situation? How do curricular actions demonstrate due
   consideration for distinct spheres of experience?
Walker: What platform beliefs underly curriculum construction?
   Through what processes is a curriculum constructed? How is the
   curriculum designed by a series of decisions? How might these
   decisions be made differently to alter and perhaps improve the
   design of a curriculum?

As representatives of the deliberative curriculum tradition, Schwab and Walker built upon the work of conventional curriculum development specialists. But their contributions also demarcate a departure from what Walker called classical models for curriculum development, bookended by Bobbitt's (1918) *The Curriculum* and Tyler's (1949) *Basic Principles of Curriculum and Instruction*. As Walker put it, relying upon theory to prescribe practice, as classical models do, assures "that practice guided by the model does what ordinary practice does, only better" (1971, 64). Tyler's use of predetermined philosophical and psychological screens to justify curriculum decisions neglects potentially generative viewpoint diversity among curriculum stakeholders. Disagreements abound regarding basic philosophical questions about what education is for. Some people accept the established social order and believe a good education teaches students according to societal norms. Others oppose extant social inequalities and believe a good education prompts students to improve the society in which they live. Further disagreements arise when addressing what it means to improve society or how and by whom social justice should be defined. Disagreements about the psychology of learning are equally abundant. Some view students as naturally curious, social, and communicative makers of meaning, while others presume students need external sources of discipline and motivation. Of course, many stakeholders maintain moderate positions, trying to avoid the potential pitfalls of ideological rigidities and uncompromising philosophical and psychological theories.

Ultimately, Schwab and Walker propose a novel conception of the relationship between theory and practice. Their deliberative tradition suggests that these disagreements should be resolved in practice, whereas classical models for curriculum development prescribe theoretical resolutions for practitioners. As Walker (1971) explained, a curriculum can be developed and designed in cold, sterile, analytical, or passionately political ways. Bobbitt and Tyler were cold and analytical. Some might even argue that Schwab and Walker were also somewhat cold and analytical because they argued for open-minded deliberations about matters of immense ethical and political significance. What should not be overlooked is that curriculum theorizing operates in varied ways. Curriculum theorizing has involved efforts to rationalize a program of study or a process for creating a program and to conceptualize or explain nuances of potentially relevant or perhaps underexamined curricular phenomena.

Seminal curriculum studies texts often address multiple facets of practice. Thus far, we have focused on the first half-century of curriculum theorizing. Tyler, Schwab, and Walker focused more on rationalizing procedures for curriculum construction than on prescribing a particular course of study. In addition, curriculum development procedures have been refined from Bobbitt to Tyler and then to Schwab in notable ways. As theorizing curriculum development evolved, these three University of Chicago theorists also conceptualized and explained curriculum phenomena with enduring relevance. For instance, Bobbitt distinguished between learning that naturally occurs in everyday life and learning that requires formalized instruction, arguing that school curricula should focus on the latter. Tyler highlighted how philosophic interpretations of knowledge, learners, and society are three main sources for determining educational objectives. Schwab distinguished between curriculum-making processes like Tyler's that were informed by theoretical inquiry and his proposal for leading stakeholders in processes of practical inquiry.

Walker (2003) identified efforts to conceptualize and explain curricular phenomena as similar yet distinctive alternatives to classical curriculum development. Efforts to conceptualize curricular phenomena do not always directly guide curriculum development but involve informing and advising the practitioners responsible for making such decisions. The way Tyler, Schwab, and Walker address curriculum goals is an illustrative example. According to Tyler (1949), learning goals depend upon the institution's (i.e., school's) psycho-philosophic screen. Walker (1971) similarly tied learning goals to explicitly or implicitly expressed platforms, while for Schwab, they are an outcome of stakeholders' deliberations. In this sense, theorists have been reconceptualizing curriculum for over a century. To illustrate, Walker (2003) points to John Dewey's work as an exemplar of theorizing that conceptualizes a practical resolution to conflicting curricular visions. Contrasting Dewey's perspective on disparate curricular visions with Tyler's, Kliebard pointed out an intractable curriculum issue. According to Kliebard (1970, 260), when faced with disparate educational and social philosophies, Dewey's "solution was not to accept them both but to 'discover a reality to which each belongs.' In other words, when faced with essentially the same problem of warring educational doctrines, Dewey's approach is to creatively reformulate the problem; Tyler's is to lay them all out side by side."

Dewey and Tyler were both aware of the competing values inherent to the coexistence of stakeholders with conflicting curriculum orientations, as were Schwab and Walker. In addition, they were all respected "progressive" intellectuals of their day. Though Dewey wrote about politics more explicitly than Tyler, they both wanted schools that orient students to democratic rather than autocratic ways of life. However, as Kliebard (1970) observed, Dewey and Tyler had very different ideas about addressing issues related to conflicting curricular visions. For Tyler, the problem of conflicting curriculum orientations must be resolved before curriculum development ensues. Valuing coherence and control, Tyler's rationale implies that someone with institutional authority needs to take control when stakeholders disagree. Tyler did not weigh in regarding who should take control or how. Rather, he insisted that consistent educational and social philosophies were a prerequisite for constructing curricula with coherent learning objectives, experiences, organizational structure, and evaluation systems. Hence, from the perspective of Tyler's rationale, when teachers and other curriculum workers encounter philosophical disputes, their primary question should be: Which philosophical position is supported by those with positional authority? Compliance is central to Tyler's advice to teachers.

Further, Kliebard observed that Dewey's advice to teachers was quite different. For Dewey, disagreements among curriculum stakeholders with diverging educational and social philosophies are an obvious societal reality. Recognizing the utility of insights from various and even conflicting interest groups, "Dewey, characteristically, treats these competing considerations as needing to be peacefully reconciled" (Walker 2003, 64). Hence, from a Deweyan perspective, curriculum construction is not merely an exercise in complying with authority or appealing to established habits, customs, or traditions. Valuing reflective inquiry and democratic ways of life, Dewey never seemed to view institutional compliance as an adequate mode of operation for teachers and other curriculum workers when they encounter philosophical disputes. Instead, curriculum workers' primary question should be: Amid our differences, what common goals and interests do we share? Representatives of the deliberative tradition of curriculum theorizing, like Schwab and Walker, contended that maintaining a deliberative ideal was preferable to compliance-based processes. Indeed, deliberative conversations are more attuned to Dewey's propensity to link democracy and education, whereas prioritizing compliance implies a more autocratic undertone.

Hence, the early 1970s marked a turning point in curriculum theorizing. Schwab, Walker, and Kliebard offered three distinct criticisms of prescriptive conventions for curriculum development. Schwab argued that curriculum construction is a practical problem that requires the artistry of practical and eclectic deliberation. Walker's main issue with the practical model is that it guides practice to do what it is already doing more effectively and efficiently, but it doesn't consider possibilities for altering the aims of practice. For Kliebard (2004), the main shortcoming of prescriptive curriculum development conventions is that they fail to address an ongoing battle among rival interest groups competing for curricular control in the United States. In addition, Kliebard (1970) criticized Tyler's rationale for curriculum development, which he referred to as the production model, for failing to acknowledge its own implicit ideological proclivities.

Questions Inspired by Kliebard

What political interest groups are competing to control your school's curricula? Which interest groups are empowered? Which interest groups are marginalized?

Several curriculum theorists have shared Kliebard's (2004) insight that curriculum is never ethically or politically neutral. Schwab's (1970) call for practical and eclectic deliberation was inspired and informed by the principles of liberal education. The arts of the eclectic involve an embrace of viewpoint diversity derived from pluralistic worldviews, disciplinary perspectives, and bodies of experience. Democratically governed secular humanism underlies the arts of the practical. Trusting deliberative conversation among equals can lead to mutually beneficial gradual reform through cooperative reasoning. The deliberative ideal, conceptualized by theorists like Schwab and Walker, is grounded in the liberal ideals often considered the foundation of modern constitutional democracies.

However, a new era of curriculum studies emerged in the 1970s. What became known as the reconceptualization of curriculum shifted the focus from controlling the development of coherent curricular programs to understanding curriculum in greater depth. According to William Pinar (2013), a leading contributor to the reconceptualization of curriculum, social reproduction, and political resistance are the two key concepts of the reconceptualization era. This presumes that dominant mechanisms of schooling in the United States, such as standard curriculum development practices, are technologies of control that reproduce extant social inequalities. When traditional curriculum development is interpreted this way, the main tasks of contemporary curriculum theory are to shed light upon and find ways to disrupt deep structures of oppression and suppression that maintain the inequitable status quo.

Several notable features became prominent characteristics of curriculum theorizing during the reconceptualization. To some extent the reconceptualization was a response to shifts in the conditions of curriculum theorizing. In the 1970s curriculum theorists generally began acknowledging that schools were no longer looking to curriculum specialists for guidance in developing and revising curricula. With recognition that they had been effectively sidelined came intentional detachments from practice, often expressed as refusals to stand above teachers and school leaders prescribing what to do and which materials to use. New ideas about what curriculum theorists do began emerging. Instead of prescribing programs of study or procedures for curriculum construction, representatives of the reconceptualization of curriculum focused on understanding and explaining the theorizing of curricular phenomena.

Another aspect of this turning point in curriculum theorizing is the prominence of criticality. With only a few exceptions, curriculum theorists became unapologetic about their overtly expressed political agendas, contrasting the open-minded liberalism of the deliberative tradition with the alleged technocratic neutrality of traditional curriculum development specialists. These shifts have involved diversifying how knowledge and ways of knowing are conceived. Reconceptualizing curriculum as an extraordinarily complicated conversation, Pinar and colleagues (1995) stepped away from everyday curricular discourse and practice conventions, promoting divergent ways of understanding what curriculum is as well as what its key elements, discourses, and practices are. In light of the reconceptualization, the intentionally planned facets of an official curriculum are only one part of curricular discourse. Embracing the fuller complexity of curricula, as the reconceptualization encourages us to do, also involves exploring curricular enactments and outcomes, which entails examining subtle aspects of hidden, implicit, and null curricula. Sometimes curricula are experienced with consequences beyond what is formally planned or even conscientiously intended. Further, sometimes what is omitted from a formal curriculum is as consequential as what is included.

Questions to Ask Yourself to Reconceptualize Curriculum

The reconceptualization imposes few, if any, boundaries to curriculum inquiry. Here are a few questions for you to consider:

- What are the curricula really doing?
- What are the various ways curricula are, can, and should be experienced?
- What experiences are concealed by conventional curricular discourses and practices?

Putting It All Together

Curricula are neither divinely created nor discovered in the natural world. Instead, they are made by people. For this reason, teachers and school leaders must carefully consider their personal and collective professional responsibilities. Making a curriculum—deciding how to represent and present the natural and cultural world in an educational situation—has been called a VUCA process: involving a volatile, uncertain, complex, and ambiguous reality. The history of modern curriculum theorizing provides a valuable framework for guiding teachers' curriculum decisions. Progressing from traditional theories for curriculum development to deliberative traditions and then to critical reconceptualizing, one gradually moves from basic curricular questions to increasingly complex forms of curriculum inquiry. Moreover, this interpretation of curriculum history highlights shifting relationships between curriculum theory and practice, another essential feature of curriculum work.

We conclude this chapter by encouraging you to engage in various forms of curriculum inquiry, reconsidering curricular concepts from the perspectives of Bobbitt, Tyler, Schwab, Walker, and representatives of critical curriculum studies. J. T. Dillon (2009) identified three interrelated types of curriculum questions: (1) questions about the nature or essence of curricula, (2) questions about the critical elements of curricula, and (3) questions about the discourse and activities of curriculum practice. Conceiving representations and presentations of nature and culture as the essence of curriculum, what are the most pressing and pervasive curricular issues in your professional context? How do your daily practices impact multiple types of curricula, such as the planned, actualized, received, explicit, implicit, and null curricula?

Walker's (1971) conceptions of curricular platforms, deliberations, and design provide a helpful framework for teachers' considerations of how they participate in curriculum practice. He referred to this as the naturalistic model for curriculum development, and it structures the HI-STAR process we will introduce in section 2. However, before moving into the HI-STAR process, our focus will turn to ways that there are possibilities and constraints on how professional educators engage in curriculum practice. In chapter 3, we highlight the possibilities for liberal, democratic curriculum practices, while also attending to the illiberal and authoritarian forces that contextualize educational practice in the United States.

3

(Il)liberal, Democratic, and Authoritarian Practices

What is the relationship between education and politics? To what degree can education be neutral, or is this an impossibility? Are education and politics inextricably linked? Perhaps the most common answer, especially among many curriculum theorists, is that education is always inherently political. Meanwhile, teachers and school leaders are typically expected to carry out practices that are not overtly political, which puts teachers in an awkward position. Yet these are only two conceptions of education's ethical and political dimensions. Educational practices cannot entirely avoid the political realm, but politicizing all aspects of education is usually not a healthy approach. Additionally, insisting on maintaining a strict boundary between education and politics also seems misguided, naive, or disingenuous. After all, schools are social institutions, and education undeniably has ethical and political dimensions. Meanwhile, the fusion of education and politics suggests that all educational stakeholders act with overt or implicit political agendas. Are students merely instruments of their teachers' politics or the politics of whoever is empowered to manage teaching practices? Are educational endeavors, in fact, synonymous with processes of indoctrination? If so, instead of distinguishing education from indoctrination, perhaps we would be well-served to cut to the proverbial chase. We needn't ask ourselves if our early-childhood centers, K–12 schools, and institutions of higher education are indoctrinating the youth. Instead, we should ask how and by whom they are being indoctrinated.

Perhaps neither a strict boundary nor an absolute fusion between education and politics is desirable. Teachers' work is animated by a very complicated relationship to the sociopolitical realm. On the one hand, decisions about the content of the curriculum and how it will be made available to students are value-laden considerations that can be altered. Noticing that there are multiple perspectives on what education's aims, goals, and objectives ought to be is merely an act of observing the obvious. Many of the most pervasive and pressing educational controversies in the United States have deep historical roots and are about conflicting curricular visions. As we described in the previous chapter, this is nothing new. Such controversies are well-documented in the literature and have been described as conflict among disparate curriculum orientations (Eisner and Vallance 1974) or political interest groups (Kliebard 2004). Of course, lists of curriculum orientations and interest groups are never comprehensive or static and are always rooted in the perspectives and understandings of the list makers at a given point in time. Vallance (1986) revised the list of curriculum orientations she previously conceptualized with Eisner, affirming the sustained relevance of her previous work and adding two additional orientations. Similarly, Kliebard's philosophical and historical insights remain relevant but should by no means be considered the "final word" on curriculum history.

Contemporary curriculum theorists continuously expand the conceptual horizons of curriculum history in the United States, and their updates are never finalized. However, for curriculum theorizing to have practical significance, it is imperative to balance the open-minded exploration of innovative, new ideas with reliance upon established ways of understanding curricula that have demonstrated sustained relevance. For instance, instead of elaborating upon the intricacies of the ideological conflicts within US curricula, Decker Walker and Jonas Soltis (2009) summarized these ongoing disputes with two succinct categories: traditionalists and progressives. While traditionalists view education primarily as a means for reproducing knowledge and culture, progressives tend to see education as a means for adapting to or even transforming social, cultural, and/or political norms. Hence, Walker and Soltis have given us categories for thinking about and discussing one of the most basic tensions in curriculum practice. Curricular aims are either grounded in worldviews that value the structure of an established order of truths (i.e., traditionalist worldviews) or informed by worldviews that believe people and society are perpetually evolving (i.e., progressive worldviews). Should a curriculum reflect a particular tradition of eternal and unchanging wisdom about what is good, true, and beautiful? Can curriculum have a blending of both? To what degree is that possible? In addition to addressing the challenging practical problems associated with the coexistence of a plurality of truth derived from diverse wisdom traditions, curriculum practice involves mediating tensions between proponents of traditionalist and progressive curricular aims. The broad category of progressivism encompasses worldviews that suggest educators should imagine and look to future possibilities when engaging in curricular and pedagogical design instead of relying upon traditions from the past. The practical implications of tensions between these conflicting worldviews create extraordinary challenges for K–12 educators.

How Are We to Proceed?

Wesley Null's (2023) book, *Curriculum: From Theory to Practice*, provides a comprehensive perspective on curriculum practice. Null insightfully suggests that curriculum practices can be mapped along two axes. His x-axis distinguishes between general or contextual characteristics of theorizing, and his y-axis differentiates between the relative trust and distrust in institutions expressed through curriculum theorizing. According to Null, clarifying these features demarcates four traditions of curriculum development, which he illustrates as a curriculum map with four quadrants. Identifying influential curriculum theorists as representatives of each tradition, Null explains four ways curriculum theorizing can be translated into practice, recognizing the unique strengths and limitations. Seeing *curriculum deliberation* as a broader term than *curriculum development*, he goes on to advance a theory of liberal education as an ideal perspective to be translated into practice that builds upon the strengths and avoids the shortcomings inherent in the four curriculum development traditions illustrated on his map. In pluralistic societies with democratic constitutions, like the United States, Null's visions for liberal education and sophisticated professional deliberations on curriculum matters seem quite sensible. It is a vision that builds upon and perhaps updates a particular tradition established by the contributions of influential curriculum theorists such as Joseph Schwab and William Reid.

In our previous book, *Democratic Curriculum Leadership: From Critical Awareness to Pragmatic Artistry* (2018), we operated from a very similar curriculum orientation. However, instead of drawing upon four traditions of curriculum development and highlighting how the deliberative tradition can mediate among them, as Null did, we focused on the tradition that dominates contemporary approaches to curriculum development. While Null reconceptualized liberal education as a theory of curriculum practice that mediates various factors related to institutional relations and theoretical character, we reconceptualized the dominant theory of Tyler's rationale for democratic curriculum leadership. Null's curriculum map in *Curriculum: From Theory to Practice* provides a helpful framework for explaining why we now believe it is imperative to shift our focus from "democratic curriculum leadership" to "anti-authoritarian curriculum practices." Further, instead of reconceptualizing Tyler's rationale for curriculum development to promote practices "from critical awareness to pragmatic artistry," we now find it necessary to introduce potentially empowering theories for teachers to use at their intellectual and moral discretion. Curriculum theorizing, as represented by the concepts and questions presented in the previous chapter, sheds light upon the multiple facets of curriculum practice that teachers encounter in their everyday practices.

From Liberal Democracy to Anti-Authoritarian Practices

Now, with reference to the evolution of curriculum theorizing in the previous chapter and Null's map, we will explain why our focus is shifting away from "democratic curriculum leadership" and toward "anti-authoritarian practices." In *Democratic Curriculum Leadership* and other works, we have recognized Tyler's rationale for curriculum development as the dominant approach to curriculum in schools (e.g., Castner 2021; Castner et al. 2020; Henderson et al. 2018; Henderson et al. 2015). Tyler's rationale is positioned in the upper right-hand quadrant of Null's map, which he called the pragmatic curriculum tradition. This means that we were identifying high levels of institutional trust and context-specific theoretical character as two attributes of dominant approaches to curriculum practice. Therefore, democratic curriculum leadership involved rethinking Tyler's rationale in ways that encourage practitioners' critical awareness of their institutional norms' shortcomings. From that critical awareness, we hoped to embolden practitioners' pragmatic artistry. In summary, we prescribed criticality and professional artistry over Tyler's neutrality and bureaucratic instrumentality.

Tyler was indeed a pragmatist, but his curriculum theorizing was what could be called an example of vulgar pragmatism (Castner 2015; Cherryholmes 1988). He referred to the psycho-philosophic screen as the basis for defining three primary sources of educational objectives. Philosophical stances and beliefs about how learning happens determine how subject matter is validated and deemed aligned with students' needs and valuable within the social world. This is an incredible insight into instrumental curriculum decisions. From a purely instrumental point of view, Tyler's rationale prompts us to consider multiple questions about the determination of educational goals:

- Should a curriculum validate so-called powerful knowledge derived from the academic disciplines of the ivory tower (Muller and Young 2019) or real-world events derived from the work of journalists and artists (Barton 2024)?

- Should considerations of students' needs and interests rely upon theory and research on how learners grow, learn, and develop, or by carefully attending to the experiences, questions, and passions students bring to the educational situation?

- Should the social value of curricular content be defined by its alignment to a way of remembering and preserving tradition, relevance to extant social situations, or propensity to inspire societal transformations?

Tyler's vulgar pragmatism evades allegiance to the specifications of any philosophical system. It can have an overly simplistic or even crude emphasis on utility and immediate practicality, often ignoring the deeper theoretical or ethical considerations. In an educational context, vulgar pragmatism can show itself, for example, in education being reduced solely to measurable, utilitarian outcomes (like job readiness or economic productivity), without regard for other important aspects like critical thinking, personal development, and so on. Therefore, Tyler's rationale for curriculum development makes no effort to answer the questions it raises.

Null's map and commitment to liberal education, on the other hand, remind us to avoid either/or thinking. Not everyone shares Tyler's trust in institutional norms, and not all theorists share Tyler's confidence in practitioners' ability to make localized decisions. Perhaps it is sometimes necessary to criticize institutions. Distrust toward authority can be warranted, and sometimes educators' decisions to work against the grain of their school's norms are justified. While localized decision-making is responsive to the particularities of specific people and situations, there are arguments that some curricular decisions can and should be uniformly controlled and even standardized by distal authorities. Null's emphasis on deliberation accounts for these diverse viewpoints for responding to and considering curriculum.

In some ways, however, Null's commitment to multi-perspective deliberation mirrors Tyler's evasion of sociopolitical allegiances. Tyler's neutrality insists the foundation of a psycho-philosophic screen must be clarified to inform practical decisions, while Null—alongside predecessors that inspired him (e.g., Schwab and Reid)—advocates for deliberative conversation as the method for determining these psycho-philosophic clarifications. For Null, the best way to make curriculum decisions is to bring together diverse stakeholders for ongoing deliberative conversations, as each offers unique and valuable perspectives based on their varied experiences. Contrasting Null's interpretation of the deliberative tradition, our conception of democratic curriculum leadership opposed Tyler's vulgar pragmatism in favor of a particular interpretation of critical pragmatism. Informed by critical pragmatism, our interpretation of the deliberative tradition in our prior book (*Democratic Curriculum Leadership* [hereafter *DCL*]) moved from critical awareness to pragmatic artistry, which positions our proclivities in the radical and existential traditions, the bottom two quadrants of Null's map.

Considering the similarities and differences between *DCL* and Null's (2023) *Curriculum: From Theory to Practice* helps explain some reasons why we are intentionally stepping away from our previous language, emphasizing "democratic" education and moving toward a new language of working against authoritarianism. The most prominent similarity between the books is that we both embrace interpretations of the deliberative tradition of curriculum theorizing, which includes the contributions of accomplished scholars such as Joseph Schwab, William Reid, Decker Walker, and J. T. Dillon. However, reconsidering *DCL* against Null's map reveals profound differences in how the two books perceive power relations in the context of curriculum practice. Null's proclivities lean toward systematic (e.g., Bobbitt) and pragmatic (e.g., Tyler) traditions of curriculum theorizing, exhibiting a level of institutional trust common among school leaders.

Our proclivities leaned toward radical (e.g., critical and postmodern theorists) and existential (e.g., Eisner's notions of productive idiosyncrasies) traditions. We embraced skepticism and idiosyncratic creativity and operated with a certain level of instinctive distrust toward institutional authorities. Therefore, instead of replacing technocratic management (i.e., Tyler's rationale) with deliberative conversation (i.e., Schwab), we reconceptualized Tyler's rationale in *DCL*. We replaced Tyler's four principles with open-ended gerunds. Instead of determining educational purposes with clearly stated objectives, *DCL* focused on professional awakening. Then, we continued reconceptualizing experiences, organization, and evaluation, focusing instead on a four-fold reflective process, including professional awakening, holistic teaching, generative lead-learning, and participatory evaluating. What we failed to consider are the many factors inhibiting professional educators' deliberative conversations and engagements in the reflective process laid out in *DCL*.

Adding these oversights to rampant concerns about the precarious sociopolitical situations threatening democracy around the globe further pushed us to consider some potential shortcomings in our previous efforts to advance democratic curriculum leadership. First, in a sense, our commitments to practical and eclectic curriculum deliberations were potentially bound by long-standing traditions of liberal education and traditions of curriculum theorizing proliferated in the 1970s. Writing from this somewhat traditionalist point of view obscures the equal validity of progressive worldviews. Second, though we emphasized pragmatic artistry, *DCL* may have still been guilty of elevating theory above practice. Moving from critical awareness to pragmatic artistry or from theory to practice can also imply a detachment from practice, a stance of producing curriculum theory for practitioners and explaining it to them to inform their daily activities. Even the very way the phrase is structured, "from theory to practice," implies this. It expresses the idea of applying abstract ideas, concepts, or knowledge (theory) in real-world settings (practice), which is unidirectional. In *DCL*, we were not sufficiently working from practice to theory nor in between practice and theory (more like practice–theory), where both mutually inform one another.

In theory, it is quite easy to idealize deliberative conversations. However, in practice, such conversations can be far more complicated because psycho-philosophic screens are not developed, nor do they exist in vacuums. Curriculum decisions are inherently political, and they occur in multiple arenas. Decisions about educational aims and purposes that teachers make for and within their classrooms interact with the regulatory mandates of school leaders and public policies. Just as there is no consensus regarding what the philosophical and psychological screens should be for determining educational goals, there is no consensus about how or even if curriculum workers should attempt to reach a consensus. Moreover, power is not usually evenly distributed among the various arenas of curriculum decision-making. When advice derived from theory informs practitioners' curriculum deliberations and invites them to consider functioning as curriculum leaders, it is imperative to recognize the potential, or even probable, constraints on deliberative conversations and professional leadership within the practical realities of schools.

Amid the intense political polarization of our day, consensus is far from likely. Agreement within and among the arenas of curriculum decision-making is so sparse that a common platform for practice is a fantasy. In recent years, traditionalists have called for the revitalization of liberal education. Some of these calls, like Schwab's, Reid's, and Null's, have been inspired by a deep appreciation for the interdisciplinary breadth of liberal arts curricula. Schwab, for example, was a biologist well known for his contributions to science education and his prominent status as chair of the University of Chicago's Great Books Curriculum. The University of Chicago has been somewhat of a de facto epicenter of some of the most ardent defenders of liberal education. Philosopher Mortimer Adler's (1982) book *The Paideia Proposal* argued for the systematization of liberal education as a remedy for what he considered undemocratic attributes of schooling in the United States. As different as his philosophy was from John Dewey's pragmatism, Adler considered himself and Dewey to be on the same page, agreeing that schools in the United States should reflect the democratic ideals expressed in the nation's founding documents. Allan Bloom's (1987) *The Closing of the American Mind* is another influential, albeit more polarizing, defense of liberal arts education. According to Bloom, the liberal arts tradition was the antidote to the alleged closed-mindedness he attributed to postmodern philosophies and various trends in progressive education.

In each of these examples, the authors did not use the term "liberal" in a partisan fashion. By calling education "liberal," they meant that broad-minded interdisciplinarity should characterize curricular and pedagogical practice, and they generally assumed that the desire for such attributes would be common among all stakeholders. Although these defenders of liberal education tend to exhibit traditionalist curriculum orientations and Dewey's progressive sensibilities were grounded in philosophical pragmatism, they worked with similar presuppositions, assuming that educational stakeholders in the United States would want curriculum leadership and schools to be democratic. However, it has become apparent that the values inherent in liberal democracy are unfortunately no longer reliably common ground among curriculum stakeholders.

In the context of culture war politics, the word *liberal* has become politicized and contentious. On the left, traditional liberal education has been criticized for perpetuating Eurocentric, patriarchal, colonialist ideologies. In addition, shifts in right-wing political ideologies have begun to include theories of a post-liberal future (Deneen 2018). This faction of "new right" conservatives rejects liberalism as a worldview that works against traditional values and shared visions of the "common good." On these grounds, Deneen (2008) has argued that Alan Bloom's vision for liberal education and Dewey's progressive philosophy of education are alike in the sense that they both envision education as a process of liberating students from their inherited traditions instead of an opportunity to strengthen their connection to the beliefs and values of a supposedly shared cultural tradition. More recent calls for revitalizing liberal education have been overtly political and have arisen from journalists rather than academics. For instance, the twenty-ninth US Secretary of Defense and former Fox News personality, Pete Hegseth, co-wrote a book entitled *Battle for the American Mind: Uprooting a Century of Miseducation* (2022). The histories of public schools, university-based teacher education, and progressive education generally are the primary targets of his criticism. Throughout the text, he alleges that progressives have controlled public schooling in the United States for over a century, and he stridently argues that these progressive educators have dismantled what he calls the "Western Christian Paideia," or WCP. Following Deneen's lead, he contends that classical Christian education, a faith-based version of liberal arts grounded in the Christian tradition, is the way to recapture the WCP.

After Democratic Education

In *DCL*, our conception of democratic curriculum leadership was inspired by John Dewey's (1934) *A Common Faith*, a book that conceives democracy as a cooperative way of life that binds together people of wide-ranging worldviews (Henderson et al. 2018). However, amid authoritarian threats worldwide, it is no longer safe to assume democratic aspirations are shared among stakeholders. There is no consensus about what education is and what it can and should do. Perhaps there never was any and maybe never will be. There is no agreement about what constitutes a quality education. What qualifies a person as well-educated? What does well-educated mean? Are education and schooling even the same thing? To what sociocultural norms should an educated person be accustomed? How, in what ways, and to what extent should educational endeavors make individual people more distinct? An innumerable variety of educational philosophies address these basic questions in divergent ways.

Many of the conditions of curriculum practice are framed by the lack of agreement on the most basic questions about the foundations of education and the heavy-handedness of many curricular decisions made in public policy arenas. This lack of consensus also extends to differing interpretations of words and phrases and their unexpected implicit and explicit meanings. For instance, politicians circulate polarizing and, at times, ambiguous and empty rhetoric, creating turmoil in local communities, schools, and classrooms. Calling on teachers and school leaders to be democratic curriculum leaders puts the onus on educators to act with greater democratic virtue than the politicians and bureaucrats enacting authoritarian practices that stifle professional artistry in education. Calls for democratic curriculum leadership presuppose that practitioners are afforded the resources to engage in professional leadership with relative autonomy. This is not often the case for educators. Considering the fragility of democracy, the conflicting visions for curriculum, and the precarity of professional leadership in education, the school and classroom-level realities of practice seem to necessitate an alternative approach.

Neil Postman (1979) argued that aspirational education theories have potentially stifled the teaching profession with their unreasonably ambitious aims. Professional educators are expected to produce educated people; they have accepted this as their primary responsibility. More prominent professions like medicine and law are not plagued with this kind of problem. Medical doctors treat illnesses rather than ensure their patients' health. Lawyers stave off injustices but cannot always guarantee justice will be realized in each and every situation. Like education, the constitution of good health and justice has been debated since antiquity. The Hippocratic Oath and habeas corpus do not promise positive outcomes. More realistically, the Hippocratic Oath promises that a medical doctor will first and foremost do no harm, and habeas corpus promises that an individual will not be unlawfully detained or imprisoned without being brought before a court of law. In this sense, doctors work against illness and pain, and lawyers work against injustices. These are promises professionals can deliver for the most part. Doctors must make sound medical decisions, and lawyers must ensure fair trials where each person is guaranteed competent legal counsel. People getting sick and sometimes dying is not a sign of malpractice.

Nonetheless, the parameters of professional education are different. Professionals are expected to promise that all their students will become educated. Supposedly, it is a sign of malpractice if this outcome is not reached. But Postman argued that educators would be wise to follow doctors' and lawyers' lead by narrowing the scope and increasing the potency of their practical aims. Provocatively, he proposes negative educational aims, conceiving of education as a painkiller. What if educational professionals paused aspirational aims to educate students for democracy and instead worked to stave off the suffering caused by authoritarian practices and various forms of stupidity? Might a focus on preventing harm and countering ignorance be more effective than striving to achieve lofty, ambiguous, and abstract educational ideals? How might the role of educators change if their primary mission shifted from idealistic goals to practical, harm-reducing aims?

Attempting to narrow the scope and increase the potency of curriculum theorizing, we will adopt Postman's advice and at least partially follow the lead of other professions. What this means is that in this book we are intentionally steering clear of conceptualizing idealized visions for democratic curriculum leadership or a liberal education suitable for a democratic society and sustaining it. Aspirational visions such as these courageously rush into the impossibilities of educational practice with unrealistic promises. Two illustrative examples are present within the four quadrants of Null's curriculum map and our reconceptualization of instrumentalized curriculum development. Asking practitioners to deliberate on the proper balance among the four categories of educational theorizing when there is no consensus in either the scholarly literature or in the public sphere puts an unfair onus on professional educators to find resolutions for matters that heretofore have entailed mystery and controversy. We do not have the last word on democratic ways of life, what constitutes an excellent education, and how curriculum practices should be oriented toward these ambitions. Moreover, as teachers are villainized in public discourse and scapegoated as the root cause of systemic social inequities, it is naive to suggest that teachers, school leaders, and educational researchers are well-positioned for professional leadership. Even if teachers, school leaders, researchers, and educational theorists had a magic wand to solve educational problems—and we most assuredly do not—prying control away from politicians who use the guise of accountability to politicize education and scapegoat an already marginalized profession is an equally complicated matter.

Therefore, instead of theorizing generative ways to enhance education through democratic curriculum leadership, we are asking you, the readers, to consider a defensive posture to mitigate the pain and suffering that is all too prevalent in classrooms today. Might a Hippocratic Oath of Education lead us to more meaningful forms of accountability? This reframing of educational practices also acknowledges the various forms of suffering many people are experiencing and asks how education can reduce such suffering. It recognizes that while educational practices are aspirational (i.e., we still want our students to experience the freedom and flourishing of robustly democratic ways of life), everyday practices (i.e., mundane experiences in schools) can, and indeed do, often cause significant harm.

Just like our counterparts in medicine, we must be mindful that our treatments or interventions can have unanticipated side effects, and sometimes, those side effects can be quite harmful. With only a few exceptions (e.g., Zhao 2018), educational research has examined the effects of instructional practices only regarding the potential benefits of an intervention. For instance, there might be convincing evidence that a particular small group reading intervention improves a facet of young children's phonological awareness predictive of reading proficiency. Of course, this is a desirable outcome. However, it is only a small part of broader goals related to supporting early literacy and overall aims related to comprehensively educating young children. In addition, it is quite possible that improving phonological awareness is not the only consequence of the intervention. Adverse consequences might accompany the measured growth in early reading skills. Some children might become frustrated if direct instruction is interfering with their playtime. Others might interpret students' participation in the small group reading interventions during a time when many of their friends are playing as a sign that they are less capable than their peers. Because such harm can often be reduced, being mindful of curricular and pedagogical side effects is vital to educational practice. While this is a very specific example, the next section considers how teachers and school leaders might consider both the positive outcomes and the potential side effects of their practices, shifting our focus from "democratic curriculum leadership" to "anti-authoritarian curriculum practices."

Even the most hopeful educators must find a proper balance between their idealistic visions and the realistic conditions contextualizing their practices. In the remaining portion of this chapter, we highlight a range of theoretical stances that can inform curriculum practice with attention to the conditions that contextualize practice. We remap traditions of curriculum practices recognizing the existence of illiberal and authoritarian practices. We supplement optimistic deliberations of practical possibilities with realistic considerations of professional responsibilities for educators to fend off potential harm caused by authoritarian practices.

The Metaphor of the Fox and the Hedgehog

Isaiah Berlin (1953) wrote an incredibly insightful essay on intellectual positioning, using the metaphor of a fox and a hedgehog. The hedgehog knows one big thing. In the threat of an attacking predator, it knows to curl into a ball and utilize its sharp quills for protection. The fox, by contrast, knows many things. Though the hedgehog is slow-moving, the fox is quick and agile. Instead of a singular approach to problem-solving, the fox adapts to the situation at hand. When confronted by a predator, the fox might run away, find a safe place to hide, or use its sharp teeth in a physical altercation. With this metaphor, Berlin provides us with a way to think about the relationship between theory and practice. Those who operate like hedgehogs rely upon great ideas or grand theories to interpret and respond to the problems of practice, while the foxes among us rely upon practical eclecticism to be responsive to situational problems on a case-by-case basis (Reid 1999).

Numerous curriculum theorists have referenced Berlin's essay. Offering a critical analysis of contemporary curriculum studies, Peter Hlebowitsh (2010) argued that foxes have overrun the field since the onset of curriculum reconceptualization in the 1970s. First, Hlebowitsh appreciates the many contributions of the reconceptualization of curriculum, describing them as a centrifugal force that perpetually diverges on how curricular phenomena are apprehended. Self-identifying as a hedgehog, he then argues for the necessity of making room in curriculum studies for the centripetal force derived from curriculum development specialists that rally curriculum studies around a common idea. This argument is reminiscent of Schwab's (1970) warning that we previously touched upon, which was about curriculum theory needing to become both practical and eclectic to avoid becoming moribund. Curriculum theorizing is ineffectual if we attribute practical contributions to curriculum development specialists and eclecticism to curriculum reconceptualization. Although scholars like Hlebowitsh are very attuned to practical problems, categorizing curriculum practice into the exclusive domain of curriculum development specialists might be hasty. Moreover, it is likely equally hasty to reduce theoretical eclecticism to the domain of university-based curriculum theorizing. Teachers and school leaders can be eclectic theorists, and university-based curriculum theorizing is itself a practice.

A deeper divide between traditional curriculum specialists and curriculum theorists since the reconceptualization lies in their attitudes toward educational institutions. Traditional theorists tend to trust institutional structures and norms, while reconceptualist curriculum theorists and beyond approach these same structures with skepticism or critical suspicion. This division reflects a broader debate over the role and reliability of institutions in shaping curriculum, as illustrated by Null's adaptation of Reid's model, which positions curriculum as an institutional force. Whereas Bobbitt and Tyler, representatives of the more traditional generation of theorizing curriculum development, were rather uncritical of the institutional norms of schooling, very few contemporary curriculum theorists believe that schools only need to become more efficient and effective at what they are already doing. According to Pinar (2013), the two key concepts that emerged from the reconceptualization of curriculum are the ideas of reproduction and resistance. In other words, schools are not, nor have they ever been, social equalizers. Instead, the institutional norms of schooling reproduce extant social inequality. From the reconceptualization onward (1970s to present), curriculum scholars have worked to understand and shed light upon the reproduction of inequalities and to advance various forms of sociopolitical resistance. The reconceptualization moved much of curriculum theorizing away from various forms of bureaucratic management and toward social and cultural issues such as inequity, social justice, critical theory, dynamics of power structure, and identity. These trends represented a shift from generally high levels of institutional trust to widespread criticism of harm caused by institutionalized norms.

Contemporary curriculum theorizing is "fox-like," as Hlebowitsh rightly observed, in that it is an intellectually pluralistic field with few, if any, decipherable boundaries. Nonetheless, curriculum theorizing might also be more like the hedgehog, designating a distinctive field of study and practice within the broader scope of educational study and practice. From this wider vantage point, traditional curriculum development specialists (e.g., Hlebowitsh) and representatives of curriculum reconceptualization (e.g., Pinar) are scholars of one big thing: curriculum, even though they often disagree about the central problems demarcating the core of curriculum studies. In this sense, many curriculum theorists may operate as hedgehogs among other hedgehogs in educational research. Specializing in curriculum studies is like other areas of specialization, such as literacy education, science education, math education, art education, social studies education, teacher education, learning science, counseling, and school administration and leadership.

Viewing curriculum as an essential element of educational practice and curriculum theory as a subset of educational theorizing, the hedgehog and fox metaphor highlights dichotomous courses of potential action. If we act like hedgehogs, we will be satisfied isolating ourselves from disparate fields of educational study and practice and engaging in specialized curricular conversations. Curriculum studies, then, is treated as one of many fragmented topics of educational study and practice. However, suppose we choose to act like foxes. In that case, we will adeptly work in an inter/trans-disciplinary fashion, highlighting relevant curricular issues and possibilities in various educational domains. Practices in literacy education, science education, math education, art education, social studies education, teacher education, and school and administrative leadership all involve curriculum work. Perhaps it takes eclectic artistry, the mindset of foxes, to adeptly consider how varied specialized fields in education are not disparate fragments but entangled pieces of comprehensive educational experience.

Remapping Curriculum Against Authoritarian Practices

With all of this in mind, we will reconsider Null's curricular map, making additions to it and shifting emphasis toward negative goals that strive to avoid illiberal and authoritarian practices. While Null (2023) centers a conception of liberal education as his curriculum platform, we based our conception of democratic curriculum leadership on a platform with seven principles: professional responsibility, critical pragmatism, circuits of valuation, the value of pluralistic humanism, folding in problem-solving, and an eclectic approach to curriculum teaching and leadership (Henderson et al. 2018). In other words, Null (2023) and Henderson et al. (2018) both offer practical curricular advice, and they begin their advising with positive curricular visions. However, this book shifts focus, adding corresponding negative goals. We argue that illiberal and authoritarian practices lead to at least four distinct types of educational malpractices that, if reduced, can relieve teachers and students from often avoidable suffering.

Along the horizontal axis, Null distinguishes curricular traditions that rely on big ideas from those that rely upon eclectic artistry. In an Aristotelian fashion, he recognizes the strengths and limitations of each. Coherence and consistency are strengths of Hedgehog's big ideas, while flexibility and compromise are the strengths of Fox's eclecticism. However, Hedgehog can be prone to ideological rigidity. Fox can become enamored with operationalism, which detaches educational practices from their moral dimensions, devolving into a relativistic form of vulgar pragmatism. Liberal education and democratic curriculum leadership require practical wisdom, achieved through careful and thoughtful deliberations. This is why Null positions curriculum deliberation in the center of the map as a "golden mean" of generalized and contextualized ways of understanding practice. In complement, the first principle of our *DCL* platform emphasizes educators' professional responsibilities to act with practical wisdom, valuing pluralistic humanism.

Conditions of Illiberal and Authoritarian Practices

What cannot be overlooked are the material realities and political conditions contextualizing practice. Examples of illiberal and authoritarian practices often hinder the conditions of educational practice in the United States. Illiberal practices, according to Glasius (2018, 517) are human rights problems that involve "patterned and organized infringements of individual autonomy and dignity." By definition, illiberal practices work against the pluralistic humanism of liberal education and democratic curriculum leadership. While positive visions for liberal and/or democratic conceptions of curricula are ambiguous in that they are open to multiple interpretations, negative visions against illiberal practices, imposing constraints on individuals' or a group's autonomy or affronts on their inherent dignity, are clear and tangible. In effect, in a pluralistic society, it is much easier and perhaps more meaningful to clarify what runs counter to the common good than it is to define elements of social cohesion and unifying principles.

Hence, expecting educators to avoid doing harm through illiberal practices is a more achievable professional responsibility than calling upon them to exhibit liberal democratic ideals that are unrealized within the sociocultural environment in which they reside.

A responsible professional educator might not be ideally engaged in deliberative processes for many reasons. Certain material conditions are necessary for teachers to engage in meaningful deliberations. To foster open dialogue and informed decision-making, key ingredients of practical wisdom, practitioners need access to relevant information and adequate time for meaningful collegial discourse and sufficient communication among stakeholders. Professional educators' deliberations can be subverted not only by illiberal practices but also by authoritarian practices. While illiberal and authoritarian practices often overlap, important distinctions exist. Instead of violating a person's or a group's human rights, as illiberal practices do, authoritarian practices interfere with democratic processes (Glasius et al. 2018). According to Glasius and colleagues, authoritarian practices are "patterns of action that sabotage accountability to people over whom a political actor exerts control, or their representatives, by means of secrecy, disinformation, and disabling of voice" (2018, 517).

A pervasive source of disinformation is propaganda, and educational situations are not immune to it. According to Neil Postman (1979, 130), "Propaganda is language that invites us to respond emotionally, emphatically, more or less immediately, and in an either-or manner. It is distinct from language that stimulates curiosity, reveals its assumptions, causes us to ask questions, invites us to seek further information and search for error." Professional educators encounter propaganda, and if they are not careful, they can spread or even construct propaganda in schools under the guise of curriculum practice. Postman warns of two types of propaganda: messages telling an audience what they should believe instead of what they should consider. The first type of propaganda is packaged in sentimentalities. *A Nation at Risk* (1983) is a prime example of this type of propaganda. Shortly after campaigning with promises to abolish the then newly formed US Department of Education, the Reagan administration created the National Commission on Excellence in Education. Under the guise of promoting vaguely defined excellence, governmental authorities utilized a mechanism of power they previously deemed illegitimate to publish a damning report on the quality of US schools. The opening pages of the report admonish the mediocrity that was/is allegedly eroding the educational foundation of US schools and ultimately putting the economic and civic future of the nation "at risk." The report framed this decline in schools as an existential threat that endangers America's competitive and cultural standing on the global stage. The report's language was intentional to mobilize public and political will for educational reform by emphasizing the high stakes for the nation if the issues of education were left unaddressed.

Unapologetically pulling out all the stops with hyperbolic rhetoric, the National Commission on Excellence in Education reframed educational reform in the United States as a national security issue. All the while, the commission's chairman, David P. Gardner, claimed the purpose of the *Nation at Risk* report was "to help define the problems afflicting American education and to provide solutions, not search for scapegoats" (National Commission on Excellence in Education 1983, iii). Further, the report expresses an appreciation for the challenges of educational practice, appreciating "the multitude of often conflicting demands we place on our Nation's schools and colleges. They are routinely called on to solve personal, social, and political problems that the home and other institutions either will not or cannot resolve" (6). Nonetheless, the report offered no solutions, and it used its authority to scapegoat professional educators for social, economic, and geopolitical problems created by corporate and political authorities. *A Nation at Risk* demonstrated a brand of propaganda that substitutes sentimentality for substantive argumentation, connecting school reform to national security.

Another type of propaganda relies upon what Postman (1979) called "surface intellectualism," which conveys the message that you can "believe this. You are being given all the information you need to know." The Global Educational Reform Movement (GERM) is filled with examples of propaganda of this sort (see Sahlberg, 2011, 2015). Data from standardized testing is presented as an irrefutable measure of school quality and teacher performance. Of course, standardized tests can produce valuable information that intelligent stakeholders can use to assess the strengths and weaknesses of their schools' programs. While it would seem obvious that scores on a standardized test provide only pieces of information, rather than everything one needs to know about what is being experienced at a particular school or in a specific classroom, test score data is often used propagandistically. The scores at this school are low. Therefore, the school should be closed due to academic failures. The scores at this school are high. Therefore, the school must have the most effective teachers in the region. This instructional strategy improves test scores. Therefore, we should implement it with fidelity and without critical reflection. This is where the propaganda of surface intellectualism and vulgar pragmatism meet. By presenting standardized test data as comprehensive indicators of school quality, educational stakeholders are steered away from deeper questions of educational purpose, equity, and well-being. The reductionist use of such data fosters narrow definitions of educational success that can lead to authoritarian practices.

Deliberative conversations must include participation from diverse stakeholders (e.g., teachers, students, milieu, subject area experts, and curriculum specialists) with unique bodies of experience and knowledge. Illiberal curriculum practices diminish the autonomy or dignity of a participant's or group's contributions to deliberative processes, whereas authoritarian curriculum practices are impositions of authority that spread disinformation or disable voice to circumvent having to justify the power and control being exerted upon others. This underscores how an environment's material conditions can nurture and support or create obstacles that hinder the deliberative ideal in curriculum practice. In addition, this reframing of curriculum practice against the threats of educational malpractices highlights the frequency of illiberal and authoritarian practices in many schools. A teacher or school leader's ideas and practical artistry are tempered by their relative autonomy and the respect demonstrated for the dignity of their practice in their professional context. One's extent of institutional trust or distrust is contextualized by the anticipated consequences of speaking and acting with ethical fidelity (Castner 2022). Telling the truth and living out one's commitments is much easier in theory than it is in practice.

There are limitations to theorizing professional responsibility as a principle of democratic curriculum leadership or centering deliberation as the "golden mean" on the vertical axis of a curricular map that dichotomizes trust and distrust in institutions. While it is usually wise to account for what schools do well and how they can be improved, the recognition of real political conditions adds another dimension to considerations of the relative trust or distrust one attributes to a school. Aristotle distinguished virtuous political conditions that govern for the common good from corrupt political conditions with self-interested governance. According to Aristotle, governance can be virtuous or corrupt whether governmental rule is carried out by one monarch or tyrant, a few members of the aristocracy or oligarchy, or the many members of a polity or democracy. The dividing line is whether governance is serving the common good or is merely for the benefit of the rulers. Hence, institutional trust is warranted when the school is governed for the common good. Distrust is justified when decisions are being made on self-serving bases. Whether curriculum policies are determined by one or a few authority figures for top-down implementation or by the many with a bottom-up strategy, the ultimate question is whether the policy serves the common good or nefarious self-interested parties. Some curriculum initiatives can be derived from popular demand. After all, children, families, and community members are educational stakeholders with invaluable voices. However, technocrats, a small group of experts with specialized knowledge, can also initiate worthwhile curriculum initiatives. Neither shared governance nor technocratic mandates are inherently good or bad. To avoid the ills of corruption, what matters is that the onus remains on the authority figure(s) using their power to make curricular decisions to justify how they exercise their authority to the people impacted by their decisions (i.e., students, teachers, and communities).

The HI-STAR Process

This section introduces the HI-STAR process—a dynamic, three-part process that guides educators thoughtfully to engage with curriculum theorizing and practicing. HI-STAR encourages a balance between visionary thinking and practical implementation. Chapter 4 explores "holistically imagining" (HI), inviting readers to envision the potential of curriculum practices while staying grounded in the realities of educational contexts. Chapter 5 moves into the "study and teaching" (ST), focusing on how these ideas come to life in practice, along with "approaches for assessing" (AR) outcomes and reflecting on growth. Together, these chapters offer pathways for educators to navigate the complexities of curriculum with criticality, creativity, insight, and adaptability.

4

Holistically Imagining Anti-Authoritarian Curriculum Practices

The intellectual, psychological, and moral demands of teaching are extraordinary. The teaching profession should be respected, and dedicated teachers should be admired. In an influential essay written over a century ago, John Dewey argued that teaching is the supreme art in any society with democratic aspirations. Admiration of teachers' intelligence and respect for the teaching profession motivated our conception of *Democratic Curriculum Leadership*. In that book, we envisioned curriculum leadership as a generous and generative form of professional artistry, and we introduced a fourfold process that intended to help practicing teachers develop professional repertoires. There is an extensive history in the United States of admiring teachers and respecting the teaching profession with links to democratic ways of life. Recognition that democracy relies upon an educated citizenry was a major impetus prompting the development of the publicly funded school system.

In educational theory, John Dewey's philosophy of education provided an important foundation for theorizing the intimate relationship between education and democracy. In *My Pedagogic Creed*, Dewey ([1897] 2017) described the complexity of teachers' everyday practice, suggesting it "marks the most perfect and intimate union of science and art conceivable in human experience. The art of thus giving shape to human powers and adapting them to social service is the supreme art"; he then demonstrated a deep respect for teachers' intellect, explaining the profession as "one calling into its service the best of artists; that no insight, sympathy, tact, executive power is too great for such service" (39–40). These observations have been implicit in over a century of theoretical contributions to advancing democratic education.

The influence in contemporary curriculum theorizing is profound. With an appreciation for the breadth and complexities of relevant perspectives, Daniel and Laurel Tanner (2007) provided a comprehensive, in-depth analysis of the historical and philosophical foundations that have informed and continue to shape curriculum theory and practice. Elliot Eisner's (1994) *Educational Imagination: On the Design and Evaluation of School Programs* further developed conceptions of educational artistry. Following the Tanners and Eisner, books like Decker Walker's (2003) *Fundamentals of Curriculum: Passion and Professionalism* and Peter Hlebowitsh's (2004) *Designing the School Curriculum* carried on these traditions providing practical curricular guidance with open-minded attention to the many coexisting beliefs and values stakeholders may bring to endeavors related to curriculum construction. More recently, McConnell, Conrad, and Urmacher (2020) provide an overview of the strengths and limitations of five approaches to curriculum design through lesson planning, providing a helpful scaffolding to practitioners looking to purposefully select the best conceptual tools for their practical context.

We have also worked within these progressive traditions of striving for democratic education amid viewpoint diversity. Our work has conceptualized curriculum wisdom (Castner, Schneider, and Henderson 2020; Henderson and Kesson 2004), democratic curriculum-based teacher leadership (Castner, Schneider, and Henderson, 2017), transformative curriculum leadership (Henderson and Gornik 2007), and the reconceptualizing of curriculum development (Henderson et al., 2015). But what if all this well-intended conceptual advice is not as constructive as we would wish? What if curriculum theorists have been overlooking vitally important realities of professional practice? Like Dewey we believe "every teacher should realize the dignity of his [or her] calling; that he [or she] is a social servant set apart for the maintenance of proper social order and securing of the right social growth" ([1897] 2017), 40). But we also don't want to presume that teachers and other readers of this text are not already acutely aware of the dignity of their practice.

Holistically Imagining Democratic Curriculum Leadership

Providing a theoretical platform for democratic curriculum leadership assumed a relationship between theory and practice oriented toward problem-solving (Henderson et al., 2018). Similar theory-practice relationships underlie Null's (2023) mapping of curriculum deliberations for liberal education and Henderson's conception of the curriculum wisdom orientation (Castner et al. 2020; Henderson and Kesson 2004). A problem-solving orientation puts theory and practice in reciprocity, which has several advantages in practice (McKeon 1952). One main advantage is the modest expectations for stable theoretical answers to vexing educational questions. What constitutes a liberal education or makes curriculum leadership democratic? How liberalism and democracy are defined depends upon who you ask. Another advantage of the problem-solving orientation is that it includes various spheres of knowledge and experience. Empirical research can inform practitioners in many ways, while teachers' proximity to students and learning experiences generates another wellspring of knowledge.

A problem-solving orientation to theory and practice is a generative way to frame curriculum practice. It embraces the necessity of ongoing reflective inquiry. Within this orientation, the deliberative ideal provides a method for making complicated and even contentious curricular decisions through rational argumentation (Walker 2022). For Aristotle, the ability to deliberate well is at the heart of phronesis (i.e., practical wisdom), and the problem-solving-orientated curriculum theorizing mentioned above generally adheres to the basic principles of Aristotelian ethics. In effect, the theories above have in common that they each aim to support practitioners (i.e., teachers and school leaders) intellectually to exercise sound judgment. Many curricular problems are complex, and practical wisdom enables professional educators to determine which educational course of action is best and beneficial given the particularities of the people and circumstances at hand.

Following Aristotle, holistically imagining education for democracy concerns practitioners' actions rather than merely cultivating a particular set of professional knowledge, beliefs, and values. Knowing about and demonstrating enthusiasm for comprehensive theories of liberal, democratic education (e.g., Ralph Tyler, John Dewey, and Paulo Freire) only matters insofar as practitioners can judiciously apply them to concrete educational situations in meaningful ways for themselves and with learners. Exercising professional judgment to enact good, beneficial practices is an endeavor that links the intellect to moral virtues, deals with particular situations rather than generalized principles, and seeks what Aristotle referred to as the golden mean. The concept of the golden mean posits that virtue is found at the mean of conflicting extremes. Thus, Null (2023) positions liberal education at the center of the extremes of institutional (dis)trust and between great ideas and eclectic artistry.

Before shifting our attention to the implications of conceptualizing curricula against authoritarianism, we will reconsider the problem-solving orientation that subtly underlies many frameworks for engaging curricula for liberal democracy. We will synthesize the contributions of numerous theorists with commitments to liberal democracy while building upon our conceptions of curriculum wisdom and democratic curriculum leadership. Then, rethinking the potential meaning of the primacy of practice, we will suggest anti-authoritarian practices as a necessary supplement to the problem-solving orientation of democratic curriculum leadership and complementary projects. To begin, we will reconsider Null's (2023) map of curricular traditions alongside Decker Walker's (1971) naturalistic model for curriculum development.

Walker's (1971) naturalistic model identifies three elements of curriculum construction: platform, deliberation, and design. According to Walker, curriculum practice always emanates from a particular platform perspective. However, multiple and sometimes competing platforms can and often do coexist within an educational situation. Null's (2023) curriculum map catalogs the infinite variety of platform possibilities into four categories: systematic, pragmatic, radical, and existential curricular traditions. The golden mean, which Null ascribes to the tradition of liberal education, is found by deliberating the ideal balance along the horizontal and vertical axes and between opposite quadrants of his map. The two axes of curriculum practice (Null 2023) are two ways of intellectually positioning practitioners within an educational situation, while the quadrants add more specificity. The dichotomies illustrated by Null's two-dimensional map are a useful scaffold for explaining the reasoning behind many commonly made decisions regarding school curricula. However, this framework does not take the conditions of practice into account.

Therefore, we will modify Null's map of practical curricular traditions to emphasize recognition of the importance of the conditions of practice. Not all pertinent curricular decisions are made within school boundaries, and stakeholders' perspectives are not always voiced with an egalitarian tone. For Null, the vertical axis signifies one's relative trust or mistrust in the institutional norms of their school. While this dichotomy of institutional trust and distrust remains essential, it is only part of how one interprets the conditions of practice. In addition to one's level of trust toward institutional norms, evaluating the conditions of practice involves appraising whether one is operating within a controlled situation or a situation that allows for or even welcomes enactments of personal and professional agency. Teachers and school leaders might ask, How am I being managed and obligated to comply with authoritative mandates? How are these obligations justified? To what extent do I trust these mandates are for the common good? Concurrently, teachers and school leaders might ask, How do I (and other stakeholders) have the agency to freely speak my mind and act autonomously in my professional context? Is this level of agency appropriate? Do I trust my judgment and the judgment of other stakeholders, or should there be greater mechanisms of regulation and accountability?

The horizontal axis characterizes the lens through which practice is experienced. Consideration of curricular issues can reference generalizable ideas or contextualized particularities. Nevertheless, it is also important to remember that curriculum practices are actualized within discourse environments, and these discourse environments can be relatively open or closed ideologically. While positioning oneself on a continuum that values the consistency of rooted thinking on the one hand and the flexibility of adaptive thinking on the other remains helpful, it is still imperative to consider the ideological conditions (i.e., curriculum workers' discourse environment) within which this sort of positioning occurs. Does the discourse environment welcome contributions from both rooted and adaptive thinkers? How does the institution deal with disparate viewpoints? Are dissenting views respected and valued? Are some ideological positions above reproach?

The dichotomies from Null's map are meaningful for interpreting the realities of curriculum practice. Often, dichotomies can be useful. They help create contrast because they present two opposing ideas, concepts, or characteristics, which can help highlight differences and distinctions as well as commonalities. However, positioning practitioners in the center of the map as rational decision-makers is a potentially misleading picture. Teachers and school leaders do not mediate curriculum practice alone, in a vacuum, unencumbered by political actors' distally made decisions. Moreover, who among us can claim to be prepared to mediate the morass of voices, choices, and perspectives that constitute curriculum practices? Further, who among us can suggest that they are adequately positioned to deliberate the golden means of extremes represented on Null's map as the outer ranges of verticality and horizontality? Conditions of power and authority are additional dimensions of curriculum practice.

Remapping curriculum practice with a third dimension adds a dichotomy of practical conditions of power and authority. On one end, the conditions are grounded in the common good, warranting compliance and actions adhering to norms. On the other end of the continuum, other interests corrupt practical conditions in ways that serve the powerful at the expense of the common good. In such cases, noncompliance and active resistance to normative expectations are justified. While compliant practices adhering to normative expectations are virtuous in conditions of polity where power and authority justify themselves to the common good, compliance is injurious in conditions of corruption, where power and authority serve themselves, unaccountable to and without regard for the common good. As Arendt argued in her book, *Eichmann in Jerusalem* (2006), extraordinary harm can be carried out through the activities of compliant, non-thinking bureaucrats. Conversely, noncompliance can be toxic when authority uses its power for the common good, but resistance is necessary and virtuous when power is a force of corruption.

Remapping Three Dimensions
of Curriculum Practice

Anti-authoritarian curriculum practices have three dimensions. The first dimension, illustrated as the x-axis, focuses on the theoretical character of curricular practices. Null (2023) described variation along the horizontal axis with the dichotomy of generalizability to contextualization. Reid (1999) distinguished between great ideas and eclectic artistry by focusing on one's intellectual positioning. These dichotomies are insights derived from classical philosophy. When great, generalizable ideas are prioritized, theory is positioned in two ways relative to practice, which Aristotelian scholar Richard McKeon (1952) called logistic or dialectical theory-practice relations. Put differently, theory either stands above practice to inform it; or theory is synthesized with practice, adhering discourse and action to a specified set of general rules and principles. However, emphasizing contextualized eclectic arts detaches theory from practice. McKeon (1952) referred to this theory-practice relationship as operationalism, which focuses on what works in the here and now rather than any general rules or principles. Null (2023) added existentialism as another philosophical possibility for contextualized eclectic artistry.

Translating these philosophical insights into the education milieu, the relationship between educational theory and practice has implications for understanding what education is and what it does. Moving left on the x-axis, education is primarily preparation for the future. The difference between logistical and dialectic theory-practice relationships is regarding the imagined future education aims to prepare students for. The logistical relationship presumes the future will or should be similar to the present and uses theory to inform the practical reproduction of the established order. The dialectical relationship imagines an improved future and synthesizes practice to this image to transform the established order. Moving right on the x-axis, education protectively nurtures the present experiences. The difference between operational and existential theory-practice relationships is regarding the locus of control. An operational relationship presumes conceptions of the common good that define what it means for practices to work well are authoritative judgments derived from institutional consensus. An existential relationship, by contrast, determines if a practice works based on whether assent is given by those upon whom authority is exercised.

TABLE 4.1

Theoretical Character (x-axis)	
Left	**Right**
Generalizable, great ideas, logistical theory informs practice; dialectical theory is practice.	Contextualized, eclectic artistry theory is operationalized according to "what works," or what works is attributed to asset.
Education is primarily preparation for the future.	Education protectively nurtures the present experiences.

Table 4.1 captures the theoretical continuum on the x-axis, highlighting how education's relationship with theory shifts based on whether it prioritizes preparation for the future or the nurturing of present experiences. Moving left, theory tends to guide practice through established frameworks that project an ordered future; while moving right, theory adapts flexibly to present contexts, emphasizing what works in real time. This spectrum helps illustrate the varying philosophical orientations toward curriculum, from traditional logistical models to adaptive, experience-centered approaches.

The y-axis creates a vertical continuum of attitudes about curriculum as a social institution. According to Reid (1999, 20), curriculum is "a socially embedded idea defined by well-known structures." Habits and traditions passed along from generation to generation and formal policy arrangements shape curricular structures. The pervasiveness of curriculum as a social institution circulates common, albeit often unarticulated, assumptions about school activities' content, purpose, and organization. On Null's (2023) map, moving upward on the y-axis signifies relative trust in the norms of curricula as an institution, whereas moving downward denotes relative distrust. Practical curriculum decisions work in ways that either adhere to, attempt to circumvent, or rebel against established institutional norms. One's relative trust or distrust in the institutional character of curricula shapes corresponding conceptions of educational purposes. For those with institutional trust, education disciplines and socializes people to maintain established sociocultural orders. However, for those with distrust, the primary function of education is to stimulate critical consciousness and unearth possibilities for social transformation.

Table 4.2 illustrates the continuum of institutional trust and distrust in curriculum as a social institution, as mapped on the y-axis. Moving upward signifies a perspective that values curriculum's role in disciplining and socializing individuals to preserve established sociocultural norms. In contrast, moving downward reflects a view that education should promote critical thinking and social transformation, challenging existing structures. This continuum helps to contextualize practical curriculum decisions within broader beliefs about the institution of education itself.

TABLE 4.2

Institutional (Dis)trust (y-axis)	
Up	**Down**
Institutional trust	Institutional distrust
Education disciplines and socializes people to maintain established sociocultural orders.	Education stimulates critical consciousness, unearths liberating growth and development, and possibilities for social transformation.

Against Authoritarianism

When asked, many teachers express attunement to robust vocational callings as a sense of intrinsic fulfillment, meaning, and personal growth rather than external factors. This strong sense of purpose is described as more than just work or establishing a career for a paycheck. For them, teaching can be like a calling that drives them to invest in preparing class experiences, building meaningful connections with students, and creating supportive learning environments. Many teachers find joy in sharing their passion for subjects in the hopes of inspiring students. Teachers' callings also often connect with their role as important for cultivating learners' minds. Teachers talk about seeing students grow and succeed, such as in those moments when they see a student's understanding 'click' with something they've been struggling with.

Moreover, experienced educators inevitably interpret curriculum practices' institutional and theoretical character in their professional contexts. It is truly rare to find an experienced teacher or school leader without well-developed opinions about what their school does well and how it might improve. These opinions often indicate discrepancies between the school's curriculum platform (i.e., the curriculum as an institution) and a personal platform comprised of an individual's beliefs and images. People and institutions can position their platforms within four quadrants along the x and y axes. Null (2023) ascribes the quadrants to four curriculum traditions: systematic, pragmatic, radical, and existential. Let's take a closer look at each one. Figure 4.1 organizes curriculum approaches into Null's four quadrants.[1] These categories, reinterpreted from Null's framework, help highlight different orientations individuals and institutions may

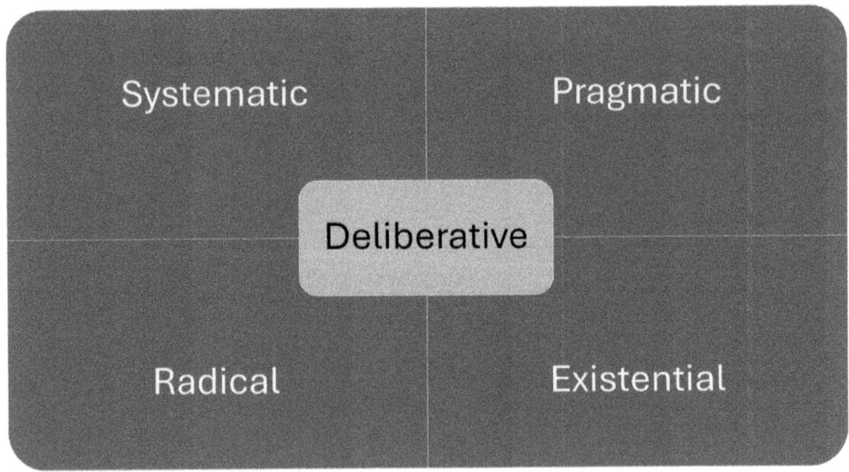

FIGURE 4.1
(SOURCE: AUTHOR)

adopt in curriculum practice. By positioning platforms along these axes, educators can better understand the alignment—or misalignment—between institutional priorities and personal beliefs, encouraging a reflective approach to curriculum development.

- The systematic tradition is in the upper-left quadrant, indicating institutional trust and an approach to theorizing that emphasizes generalizable, centrally controlled curricular prescriptions that preserve institutional traditions.
    - **Conceptual and operational definitions of education:** Education is preparation for the future. It disciplines people to maintain established sociocultural orders.
    - **The source of curricular aims and methods:** Determining the aims and methods of education is fundamentally a scientific question. This underscores the importance of evidence-based practices. We must implement our best science, which will evolve.
    - **Common examples in curriculum theory:** Bobbitt, Snedden, essentialist philosophies of education (e.g., E. D. Hirsch's Core Knowledge).
    - **Common examples in curriculum practice:** Teacher-directed explicit instruction and behaviorism; Science of Reading and other evidence-based practices; the What Works Clearinghouse (WWC) endorsed by the US Department of Education and the Institute for Educational Sciences (IES).
- The pragmatic tradition is in the upper-right quadrant, indicating institutional trust and an approach to theorizing that emphasizes contextualized and locally controlled curricular prescriptions.
    - **Conceptual and operational definitions of education:** Education responds to current sociocultural conditions to construct coherent and controlled educational plans.
    - **The source of curricular aims and methods:** Determining the aims and methods of education is fundamentally a philosophical question. People disagree but can or indeed must determine a shared philosophical foundation to develop coherent and controlled curricula.
    - **Common examples in curriculum theory:** Tyler's rationale, Understanding by Design (see Wiggins and McTighe 2005), Universal Design of Learning (see Meyer, Rose, and Gordon 2014).
    - **Common examples in curriculum practice:** Local interpretation of best practice and operationalism via instructional management or leadership.

- The radical tradition is in the bottom-left quadrant, indicating institutional distrust and an approach to theorizing that emphasizes generalizable, centrally controlled curricular prescriptions that transform sociopolitical norms.
  - **Conceptual and operational definitions of education:** Education liberates people in unjust social conditions and unearths possibilities for social transformation.
  - **The source of curricular aims:** Determining the aims and methods of education is fundamentally a philosophical question. People disagree but can or indeed must determine a shared philosophical foundation to develop coherent and controlled curricula.
  - **Common examples in curriculum theory:** Transformative consciousness-raising and critical pedagogies (e.g., Paulo Freire, Michael Apple, Henry Giroux, bell hooks).
  - **Common examples in curriculum practice:** Any form of educational activism. Due to the politicization of education in the United States, a comprehensive list of examples is beyond the scope of this chapter. However, there are numerous examples of educational activism with both left-wing and right-wing political agendas. While contemporary curriculum scholars/activists almost exclusively operate from the left, educational reform policies are almost uniformly right-wing.
- The existential tradition is in the bottom-right quadrant, indicating institutional distrust and an approach to theorizing that devalues the establishment of predetermined curricular prescriptions in favor of individualized autonomy.
  - **Conceptual and operational definitions of education:** Education is a process of becoming. It nurtures people in their present environment, enabling them to develop/become their best selves.
  - **The source of curricular aims and methods:** Determining the aims and methods of education is fundamentally a personal question, pertaining to an individual's development growth or existential becoming. This underscores the importance of individualization. What is a good education for one individual or group might be harmful to others.
  - **Common examples in curriculum theory:** Psychoanalytic theories (e.g., Carl Jung), autobiographical inquiries, radical constructivist experiential learning, and aesthetic approaches to curriculum design (Moroye and Uhrmacher 2009), experience-based objectives (Ingman and Moroye 2019).
  - **Common examples in curriculum practice:** Student/child-centeredness, de/un-schooling.

- The deliberative tradition is in the center of the map, indicating that it is the ideal balance of the four quadrants. However, deliberation is a (but not the) method for making curricular decisions. In addition to deliberation, teachers and school leaders can employ nonreflective, technical-managerial, conflict-oriented, and peace-oriented approaches to curriculum practice.

In some ways, providing them with conceptual frameworks to scaffold the development of their professional repertoires and practical decisions falls flat. While such frameworks can be helpful scaffoldings for teachers' reflections and deliberative conversations, it is equally important to consider the conditions of educational practice. There are numerous barriers to teachers' professional autonomy. While it may be tempting to consider our current political polarization and dramatically contentious school board meetings unprecedented, teachers have been caught in the middle of curricular conflicts for decades. In 1990, Hlebowitsh wrote about the various forces obstructing teachers' professional artistry.

Today, teacher intelligence is being quashed by various instructional mandates that have the effect of narrowing the curriculum in the classroom. Many of these mandates are sanctioned by the educational leadership as proper and acceptable professional conduct. They arrive at the schoolhouse door through the exercise of special interest pressures by various agents, including the political leadership, the textbook publishing industry, the media, and the testing industry. (1990, 150)

Mandates from policy arenas and school leaders can present significant obstacles to teachers making optimal practical decisions. Fickle professionals do not cause pendulum swings in educational policy and practice. Instead, as Hlebowitsh explained, authority figures outside the classroom frequently generate patterns of change in curricular discourse and action. In the United States, curriculum practices are frequently managed from the top down. Enhancing teachers' conceptual clarity is not all that the realization of professional artistry requires. Many actions taken in schools are not the outcomes of teachers' deliberations, and external authorities frame many school-level deliberations. Therefore, attributing all or even most curricular decisions exclusively to the sophistication of teachers' will and skill—suggesting that all or even most problems could be solved if teachers balanced their interpretations of the institutional and theoretical character of curricula—misinterprets (or even wholly overlooks) the conditions characterizing many teachers' professional contexts.

At the same time, this is not to say that all systematic regulations hinder pedagogical artistry. The critical question is not so much about whether power and authority are exercised in curriculum practice. This is an inevitable and unavoidable feature of education. However, central questions about the conditions of curriculum practice focus on the legitimacy of power and authority. If authority is legitimate, how and by whom is authority legitimized? When power is exercised in an educational situation, is the person or group of people exercising power accountable for justifying their power and authority to those affected by their actions? These differences are what distinguish authoritarian conditions from more liberal, democratic situations.

The conditions of practice reflect social, political, and cultural patterns that are often beyond professional educators' direct control. In other words, teachers do not choose or create many of the conditions of their practice. Often, as Hannah Arendt reminded us, they might wish societal norms were different than they are. Educators view sociopolitical values as foundational elements of their curricular platforms. However, here our focus is on professional educators' view of the politics of their curriculum practice rather than their broader sociopolitical beliefs and values per se. Recalling Reid's (1999) conception of curriculum as an institution, the key questions on the z-axis focus on how the norms of curriculum practice reflect the principles of open or closed societies.

An open society reflects the principles of liberal democracy, while a closed society has authoritarian features. In an ideal situation, the conditions of practice reflect an open society. Such a situation affords professional opportunities to find an intelligent balance among the four quadrants of Null's (2023) map. Yet, considering how pursuing wisdom and democracy are aspirational endeavors rather than demonstrative goals, it is important to avoid putting unrealistic expectations upon teachers. This is not to say that countless teachers are not doing extraordinary work with profoundly democratic sensibilities in their classrooms and schools with students. Many teachers certainly have been and are doing such work. Nonetheless, utopian visions without materialized exemplars are poor foundations for practical decisions. What does it mean to say a person is well-educated? What does it mean to help someone become well-educated? What conditions foster personal growth and social responsibilities in a democratic society? What does it mean to say that an educated person is prepared to be a contributor to a democratic society? What does that even look like? These questions are open to multiple interpretations, and people address these questions in disparate ways.

For these reasons, we will follow Postman's advice to narrow the scope and sharpen the focus of our efforts. We do this by differentiating between the deliberative ideal characteristic of an open society and authoritarian practices that permeate a closed society. Susan Nieman (2023) noted three principles of modern liberalism. These are signals of social, cultural, and political conditions reflecting an opened (or at least an opening) society.

Nieman contrasted these principles with illiberal ways of thinking, which she warns are becoming increasingly prominent worldwide. Hence, at least philosophically speaking, Nieman dichotomizes open and closed social conditions according to three features. First, virtuous conditions strive for the common good, premised on the idea that all people possess universal and equal dignity. Second, while there are often palpable relationships between justice and power, these are two distinct concepts. Third, progress is possible, although it is never inevitable. Nieman's warning is that tribalistic interest groups, conflations of justice and power, and doomsday pessimism that render progress impossible present a corrupted alternative to the principles of liberal, open societies. Anti-authoritarian curriculum practices involve refusing to think, speak, and act in accordance with the attributes of a closed society.

In table 4.3 we contrast the attributes of an open society with those of a closed society, as articulated by Nieman.

In an open society, values such as universal dignity, the distinction between power and justice, and the belief in possible progress are emphasized. In contrast, a closed society is marked by tribal interests, the conflation of power and justice, and a pessimistic view that progress is futile. These distinctions underscore the philosophical divide between educational practices that support democratic ideals and those that reflect authoritarian tendencies.

Departing from our previous work, instead of conceiving education as cultivating wisdom and advancing democratic ways of life, we take up Postman's conception of education as a painkiller. As a painkiller, education has incredible potential to relieve the suffering of individuals and groups that has sadly become a persistent and pressing feature of life in the United States. For Postman (1988), education fends off the pain caused by the various forms of stupidity circulating within our social discourse. Similarly, we view curriculum practice as having the serviceable potential to fend off harm caused by various forms of illiberal and authoritarian curriculum practice.

TABLE 4.3

The Conditions of Curriculum Practice (z-axis)	
Signs of an Opening Society	**Signs of a Closing Society**
Universal dignity and equality [common good]	Tribal interests [interest group]
Power and justice [authority can be legitimate or illegitimate]	Power is justice [might makes right]
Progress is possible but not inevitable [education can improve lives if it is done well]	We are forever doomed and caught in a power situation [education is a perennial power struggle]

Postman argued that we will never live in a world without stupidity. As he conceived it, stupidity is a discursive action, not a dispositional attribute. Therefore, Postman did not propose methods for identifying or reprimanding stupid people. Instead, he focused on how everyone participates in discourse and is, therefore, susceptible to painful experiences with stupidity, whether they are the recipient or perpetrator of stupid talk. Unfortunately, harmful illiberal and authoritarian practices will probably always exist, just as illness, injury, suffering, and social injustices are recurrent realities of our social world. The difference is that doctors and lawyers are not expected to produce a utopian vision. It would be preposterous to suggest that illness and injustice result from doctors' and lawyers' incompetence. Moreover, profit motives and the politicization of the medical and legal systems in the United States corrupt the conditions of medical and legal practice. Medical and legal professionals work within imperfect conditions, and they are not merely technicians. There are critical moral dimensions to their practice, and professionals must accept moral responsibilities to ensure their discourse and activities are not co-opted by nefarious interests. First and foremost, they are individually obligated to avoid perpetuating harm.

Similarly, the abundant anti-intellectualism and disparities in schools in the United States are not a sign of professional educators' incompetence. Schools have been politicized for decades, and like doctors and lawyers, educators work in very imperfect conditions. Also, like medicine and law, education has a moral dimension. This is why school curriculum has become a central issue in the contemporary culture war. Conceiving teaching as a merely technical endeavor reduces education to mere training or, worse, indoctrination. For this reason, it is vitally important for professional educators to reconsider what promises their curriculum practices can deliver. Teachers cannot promise their students will experience democratic goodness, just as doctors cannot promise health to their patients, and lawyers cannot promise justice to their clients. Nonetheless, professional educators can promise to individually do no harm, as doctors and lawyers do. As professionals, educators must take on the moral responsibilities related to protecting curricular discourse and activities from the forces of corruption that surround them.

In other words, suggesting professional educators can promise experiences of democratic goodness lacks important validity criteria. The first criterion is meaningfulness. There is no universal understanding of what constitutes a democratic experience, and what it means to pursue democratic virtue has been contested since antiquity. Who are we, as authors of this text, to attempt to define democratic goodness for the readers? Such an attempt would seem to be a profoundly undemocratic thing to do. The second criterion is logical consistency. How can educators promise their students what they cannot assure for themselves? The third criterion is factual validity. Providing theoretical guidelines for curriculum deliberation presupposes that professional educators are empowered to choose among a variety of curricular possibilities with relative autonomy. Often, this is not the case.

A more meaningful, logically consistent, and factually valid premise is that many (if not most) educational situations include illiberal and authoritarian curriculum practices (i.e., educational malpractices). We all experience the harmful effects of these practices, and professional educators can reduce suffering by staving off harm caused by educational malpractice. Curriculum practices are discourse, and activities occur within social, cultural, and political contexts. The relationship between practice and conditions is dialectical. Curriculum practices do not shape but can influence social, cultural, and political conditions. While social, cultural, and political norms inescapably affect curriculum practices, practitioners needn't be passive recipients of these disparate and sometimes conflicting influences. As illustrated by the y-axis, practitioners who trust institutional norms accept the prevailing patterns of social, cultural, and political influence. Meanwhile, practitioners who distrust institutional norms may resist or refuse those same patterns of influence.

Because authority can be justified, but not all existing forms of authority are justifiable, practitioners should take a nuanced position on institutional trust and distrust. Fully trusting the curriculum as an institution, especially without adequate justification, is naive. But fully distrusting the norms of school is pessimistic and potentially reckless. Moreover, in some cases, theoretical generalizability anchors commitments to universal truths and values, such as the equal dignity of all people. In other cases, theoretical generalizations are the roots of dogmatic intolerance. Contextualization, on the other hand, can generate adaptive problem-solving or morally ambiguous operationalism. There are things schools do well and even instances where students and teachers experience a virtuous polity (i.e., democratic goodness). However, schools are also problematic places where the common good is corrupted by unaccountable authority figures (i.e., authoritarians), who often distort universal truths and values, sabotage accountability for how they exercise power and subvert possibilities for social progress (i.e., tenets of liberal democracy). While democratic education is an aspirational vision, elements of a closed society are tangible features of educational experiences in the United States. For this reason, we holistically imagine a three-dimensional vision for anti-authoritarian curriculum practice.

Mapping a Third Dimension of Curriculum Practice

The conditions of practice (i.e., the z-axis) underscore the positive and negative forces influencing curriculum work. Even from the perspective of pure positivity, curriculum deliberations are very complicated. Curriculum leaders are stakeholders who work alongside other stakeholders (e.g., students, teachers, subject area experts, and social, political, and cultural representatives) to deliberate their curriculum's purpose, content, and organization. Their focus is on the people and context of a particular situation, and their case-by-case decisions determine how practices are enacted. Finding an optimal balance among the four curricular traditions is an unending quandary. In other words, curriculum deliberations are a perpetual rather than a periodic component of practice. Deliberations require remaining adaptive, responsive, and reflective.

Even the most experienced educators sometimes misjudge the demands of a given set of circumstances and must reconsider their decisions. Such occurrences are inevitable. Given the multitude of factors influencing the elements and operating procedures of curricula, it is imperative to recognize the dynamic nature of curriculum work. Curriculum deliberations are not processes that produce finished products. Instead, they are processes oriented for ongoing adaptive problem-solving that respond to the fluid demands of educational situations. The responsiveness of a teacher, student, subject area expert, community member, or curriculum leader) to other stakeholders' ideas, interests, and concerns is a signpost of professional artistry in education. In sum, professional artistry is a creative, relationally responsive way of approaching curriculum practice that requires immense intelligence, imagination, compassion, and ingenuity.

While the need for educators to engage in adaptive problem-solving may seem obvious, conditions of curriculum practice are often less than conducive to educational professionals' meaningful deliberative processes. Significant obstacles often constrain teachers' and school leaders' professional artistry. In many ways, these obstacles are rooted in dominant perceptions of the relationship between educational authority and accountability, which reflect a closed society's attributes. Whether operating within the classroom, a school or district leadership team, or the public policy arena, making practical decisions about curriculum is an exercise of authority. Although authority can be and, to some extent, is exercised in classrooms, schools, and policymaking, power is usually not evenly distributed among these arenas. In the United States, a clear hierarchy imposes a top-down structure upon curriculum practice and thus on teachers.

Teachers are the adults with the most proximal relationship to curricular enactments. They mediate the content and purposes of the curriculum pedagogically to optimize students' experiences at school. When discrepancies exist between the planned and received curricula, teachers are best positioned to notice and respond if needed. School leaders, such as building principals and central office administrators, may have a bird's-eye view of their school or district. Still, they do not have the teachers' proximal perspective on students' experiences, which Dewey (1938) observed can be educative, noneducative, or mis-educative experiences. Nonetheless, teachers' professional authority is typically subordinate to school leaders' authority, who, in turn, are subordinates to policymakers' mandates. In the United States, a nation that prides itself on the absence of regulations imposed by centrally controlled national curricula, educational authority ironically increases as it becomes more distal to practice.

The absurdity of power and authority increasing with its distance to practice has distorted notions of accountability in US education. Policymakers frequently make important curricular decisions *for* rather than *with* or *by* teachers and school leaders. This is not necessarily forbidden in an open society. On some matters, the expansive view of an official working within a state department of education may be quite helpful, and standard regulations across an entire state can be beneficial. However, a state-level bureaucrat is far too detached from the enacted curriculum to make intelligent decisions regarding several facets of curriculum decision-making. Moreover, many have never spent time in a classroom teaching students, which seriously limits their understanding of the day-to-day of teaching. This distance can lead to decisions that overlook the practical realities and nuanced needs of individuals, classrooms, and schools, resulting in policies that may lack relevance or effectiveness.

Again, the issue is not that there is something inherently wrong with power being exercised in the public policy arena. On the contrary, such authority is often justifiable and even necessary. However, the value of a decision is not determined by the authority of the entity making the decision. Influential policymakers and school leaders can be ill-informed or uninformed about relevant factors of an educational situation. Therefore, the issue is that the authority is exercising power while sabotaging accountability, rendering themselves unaccountable for the consequences of their actions. This is an authoritarian practice. In fact, for decades, policymakers have distorted notions of educational accountability in the public discourse by using their authority to make curricular decisions. Instead of being answerable to stakeholders for those decisions, policymakers promise their constituency to hold teachers and school leaders "accountable" for the consequences of public policy decisions. Thus, the contemporary discourse of educational accountability is, in fact, accountability sabotage.

In the United States, school leaders encounter authoritarian practices. When school leaders employ instructional management strategies, they often respond to policymakers' accountability sabotage with their own authoritarian practices. Because authoritarian practices are potentially harmful and commonly lead to educational malpractices, teachers must avoid two very ordinary entrapments that perpetuate authoritarian practices in the classroom. If teachers have uncritical trust in the curriculum as an institution, they may find comfort in having complicated curricular issues decided for them. On the other hand, teachers with unwavering distrust in the curriculum as an institution may become unreasonably strident in their opposition to authority. When educators operate as bureaucratic functionaries or political reactionaries, they can and often do pass along the harm of authoritarian practices they are victims of to their students.

Teachers and school leaders often encounter situations where accountability for curricular decisions made in public policy arenas (i.e., top-down curriculum reform mandates) has been sabotaged. In other words, policymakers frequently obligate schools to implement a particular program or instructional strategy (or type of program or strategy) while also promising to hold teachers and school leaders "accountable" for the fidelity of implementation and/or outcomes. Under such conditions, teachers are blamed for not implementing the mandate properly if it is ineffective or has unanticipated negative consequences. Accountability sabotage renders it impossible to consider that the policymakers misused their authority or made a dumb decision. These situations call for teachers' and school leaders' anti-authoritarian curriculum practices.

There are two layers of anti-authoritarian curriculum practices. The first layer, which precedes deliberations envisioning curriculum improvements, is a careful appraisal of the potential risks involved in curricular decisions that have already been made, including decisions distal authorities may have imposed upon local stakeholders. Envisioning curricular change is only serviceable when it recognizes that curriculum work is never carried out in a vacuum, and it rarely begins with a blank canvas. Some decisions have been made with authority that bind how curricula will be designed and actualized in the realities of practice. Nonetheless, teachers and school leaders exercise authority at the classroom and school levels. Though professional educators do not enjoy unfettered professional autonomy, there is a second, more generative layer of anti-authoritarian curriculum practice. Teachers and school leaders mediate educational policy and theory, transforming curricular plans into everyday practical discourse and action. Before curricular ideas are actualized, practitioners accept, reject, or reinterpret theoretical and policy prescriptions. Hence, there is a second layer of anti-authoritarian practice focused on mitigating the potential harm caused by decisions practitioners did not make, may disapprove of, and may privately or overtly hope to change.

Bureaucratic functionaries accept the risks of harm as part of the natural order of things and beyond the scope of their control and responsibilities. Strident reactionaries, in their zeal to counteract the risks of harm created by authoritarian practices, can create additional risks if they sabotage accountability for their actions and reactions. Therefore, holistically imagining anti-authoritarian curriculum practice is intentionally inactive. Before springing into action, it is important to consider the full scope of the conditions of curriculum practice, including one's own positioning and influence within their professional context. Recognizing that the wisdom needed to realize democratic education has been elusive since Socrates and the marginalized professional authority ascribed to educators, anti-authoritarian curriculum practice then reduces the scope of educators' holistic imagination. Curriculum workers' foremost responsibility is to do no harm. Identifying the types of educational malpractice (i.e., harmful manifestations of authoritarian practices that corrupt the conditions of curriculum practice) is the first step in mitigating such risks.

Educational malpractice has four main categories, mirroring the four traditions of curricular engagement discussed above. When accountability sabotage corrupts the conditions of practice, the potential strengths found within each of the four quadrants of the two-dimensional map become distorted. At their worst, the negative consequences are many, as depicted in figure 4.2:

(1) Systematic programs and evidence-based instructional plans become scientism when methodologies mirroring the natural sciences are the only form of inquiry used to address educational problems. Educational practitioners are reduced to technicians who work with data instead of people.

(2) Locally defined best practices become faddism when educators futilely look for panaceas. Deferring to a combination of distal authorities, school leaders codify a collection of so-called "best' practices without any firm ethical commitments.

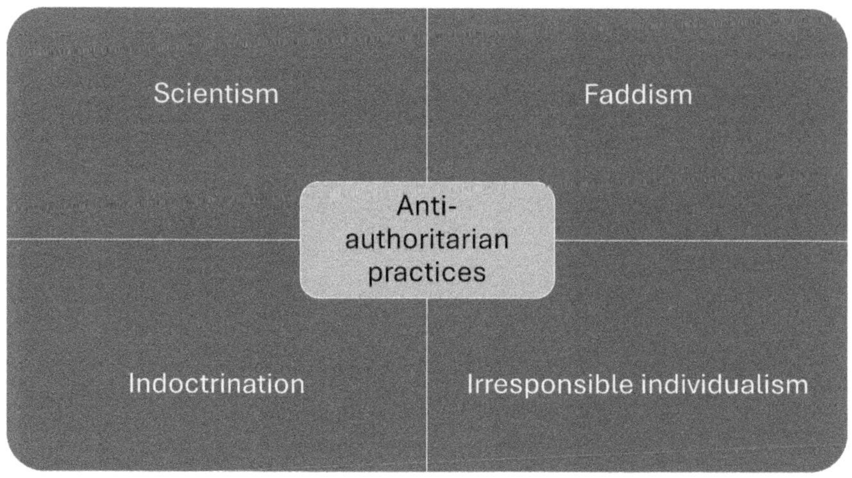

FIGURE 4.2
(SOURCE: AUTHOR)

(3) Educational advocacy becomes indoctrination when educators replace a dominant ideology with an alternative ideological vision. Educational practitioners' battles for control replace reasonable compromise and earnest struggles for freedom and justice.

(4) Individualized student-centered approaches become irresponsible individualism when teachers and school leaders relinquish their authority (and responsibilities) to students. Educational practitioners become permissive observers in pedagogical situations, rendering everyone unaccountable to the common good.

In this chapter, we have holistically imagined (HI) anti-authoritarian curriculum practices. Next, we shift from the theoretical focus to study, teaching, assessment, and reflection (STAR) activities. Professional artistry is a creative action. It is about judiciously choosing when to enact compliance, reinterpretation, resistance, and refusal.

5

Study, Teaching, Assessment, and Reflection (STAR)

In the previous chapter, we highlighted an important exercise in educational theorizing, analyzing the methods and conditions of curriculum practice and imagining what we can and should do and what we cannot or should not do. According to MacDonald and Purpel (1987, 192), curricula "emerges from an orientation and a vision of who and what we are, where we come from, and where we are going. What is of the most extraordinary import, of course, is which particular vision we decide to choose, for the choosing of a vision allows us to become that vision."

Professional educators have arrived at a fork in the road, and they have vital choices to make. However, they are not only making decisions regarding their platform orientations. Curriculum work also involves situating oneself and one's vision within the realities of one's professional context. As standardized instructional management and authoritarian practices pervade contemporary conditions of curriculum practice in the United States, curriculum work is more complicated than merely choosing a vision for oneself and striving to become that vision in practical discourse and action. The other side of curriculum work involves negotiating the various and often conflicting educational visions coexisting within one's professional context. Cooperative deliberations among conflicting curriculum orientations can be challenging even under egalitarian conditions. Yet, most school contexts are not egalitarian, and teachers are routinely subordinated to more distal authorities.

We shift our attention from the inactive processes of holistically imagining curricular visions to four practical actions: study, teaching, assessment, and reflection (STAR). Put differently, holistically imagining (HI) curricular platforms are theoretical practices. It involves analyzing the methods and conditions of curriculum practice and envisioning what one can and should do and what one cannot or should not do. Many professional educators tacitly engage in the internal process of holistically imagining curricular possibilities. However, they are too infrequently invited to discuss or enact their visions within typical structures of schooling. Because one's educational imagination does not directly impact the material world, it can be kept private and even go unnoticed. Educators directly impact the concrete realities experienced in classrooms and schools when they speak and act with professional authority. Teachers exercise authority through the practical arts of study, teaching, assessment, and reflection (STAR).

Study Implications for Professional Educators

Professional study is an empowering practice. Most pre-service and practicing teachers and school leaders engage in academic study and ongoing professional development throughout their careers. Being a student of education involves explorations of educational theory and research as well as experiential learning. To some extent, experiential knowledge about education is ubiquitous. We have all had educative experiences as students, and our experiences shape our views on what content and purposes should be prioritized and why. We suspect many readers of this book also have teaching experience. It is difficult to exaggerate how significant practical experience is. Experiential learning is a critical component of most teacher preparation programs. It is not uncommon for preservice teachers to report disconnects between what they are learning in their courses and what they are observing in the schools. Experienced classroom teachers are often very knowledgeable about the inner workings of their schools. With this knowledge, they can usually quickly evaluate the serviceability of educational theory, policies, and programs in their professional context.

In many cases, there is a chasm dividing theoretical and practical knowledge. Imagine the following hypothetical discussion among three university-based teacher educators:

- Professor 1: Our students complain that their professors have never been teachers or have been out of the classroom for too long. They say that we are unaware of what is happening in schools.

- Professor 2: That is because of a lag in implementation. The most up-to-date research always takes a while to reach classrooms. I hope our students can help educate their mentor teachers on evidence-based practices, or perhaps we can begin working more directly with the schools.

- Professor 3: We are very aware of what is going on in classrooms and are introducing our students to alternative and more meaningful approaches to teaching. The status quo in schools is horribly unjust!

So, hopefully, some of our students will be open-minded enough to advocate for changes when they start their teaching careers.

To their credit, these fictitious characters each validated their students' observations that they were being exposed to conflicting educational visions. Nonetheless, they demonstrate three common types of deficit-mindednesses. The students and the professor initiating the conversation assumed that the knowledge deficit was derived from the university faculty's geographic and/or temporal distance from practice. The professors who responded turned the table, suggesting the knowledge deficit was in the schools. Although they expressed two different hypotheses about the nature of the deficiency, they shared the presupposition that theory and research produced at the university should inform practice.

Professor 2 presupposed a relatively cooperative relationship between university-based theory and research and P–12 practice. Considering everyone to be generally on the same page, this professor viewed university-school communication as the best way to bridge the divide. Professor 3 instead assumed a more adversarial relationship with P–12 practices. This professor perceived our students to be observing conflicting curricular visions. While the second and third professors interpreted news of the students' observations differently, they shared the inclination to suggest that practical issues can and should be rectified by experts' ideas. Little if any attention was given to the possibility that other stakeholders (e.g., students, teachers, community members) had valid contributions to consider.

This inclination implies two types of narrow aims for teacher education curricula. Positioning oneself as an expert possessing the knowledge practitioners need, as Professor 2 and Professor 3 did, suggests that accreditation and socialization should be the basis for curriculum aims in teacher education. This means, on the one hand, that curricular goals are defined as a prespecified set of knowledge, skills, and dispositions for experts to transmit to preservice and practicing teachers (i.e., aims of accreditation). Then, on the other hand, Professor 2 implied that practicing teachers should be introduced to the norms of the most up-to-date evidence-based practices, and Professor 3 argued that teacher education should socialize preservice teachers to be advocates for institutional change (i.e., aims of socialization). Interestingly, these colleagues expressed different perspectives on the ends of socialization. Professor 2 presumes practitioners are generally heading in the right direction and need to be socialized to work with greater efficiency or effectiveness, but Professor 3 wanted to alter the direction of practice altogether.

According to Biesta (2024, 4), the aims expressed in this hypothetical conversation must also account for students' "subjectification," or they are not fully educational. For aims to be fully educationally oriented, they must signify that teachers and school leaders are "interested in students' independence, that is, in providing each student with a fair chance at being the subject of their own life, rather than the object of what others—whether individuals, groups, or more abstract forces such as capitalist social media—may want them to be and do."

Whether focused on early childhood education or professional education, curriculum practices often need to do many things. An intentionally designed educational experience often carefully considers what students will know, understand, and be able to do (i.e., accreditation) after participating in this educational experience and how they will be inducted into the social, political, and institutional norms (i.e., socialization). Training and indoctrination are also intentionally designed programs with clearly defined accrediting and socializing aims. Education contrasts training and indoctrination by nurturing students' growth of independent minds, bodies, and spirits. At least in part, education is a journey of discovering oneself, the world, and how one is being positioned and may wish to reposition oneself in the world.

As discussed in the previous chapter, curriculum practice (i.e., discourse and action) involves considerations of institutional trust or distrust, theoretical character, and the conditions of practice. As precarious as the sociopolitical conditions of life and the status of professional education might be in the United States, what professional educators say and do matters intergenerationally. While reflective inquiry practices are generative for life in an open society, authoritarian practices contribute to a closed society. Teachers and school leaders' ability to engage students in meaningful reflective inquiry that provides "each student with a fair chance at being the subject of their own life" depends upon the intellectual independence they realize in their own life, personally and professionally. One is not cultivating anti-authoritarian sensibilities in the next generation if adherence to authority is the only criteria they use to validate the quality of their practice.

The first component of the STAR process is professional **study**. Educators learn and grow throughout their careers, and how they approach curricular and pedagogical study and practice cannot be fully controlled under any conditions. Professional artistry involves six forms of practical and eclectic reflective inquiry. Maintaining practical eclecticism in contemporary American schools is often tricky because authoritarian practices pull teacher education, which includes professional development, toward various forms of malpractice. Teachers and school leaders must frequently compromise their professional artistry to comply with institutional mandates. While such compromises are understandable and arguably sometimes necessary, if professional artistry is sacrificed, compromise turns into corruption. Educational malpractices corrupt curricula into propaganda and pedagogy into indoctrination.

Engaging in eclectic curriculum study is an anti-authoritarian practice that fends off manifestations of propaganda. Eclectic curriculum studies involve at least six forms of inquiry, including practical, personal, critical, communicative, dialectical, and ecological inquiries.

- **Practical inquiry:** Problem-solving is emphasized in practical inquiries. It addresses the real-world, everyday challenges specific to a particular state of affairs. Deliberate decisions are a pragmatic outcome rather than prescriptions, descriptions, and explanations. To get started one might ask questions such as: What issues/problems do I want to better understand/address? What can be improved? What are some of the potential ways I might begin to explore issues/problems? What might be (or are) potential consequences?

- **Personal inquiry:** Introspection, personal choices, individual responsibilities, and the search for authenticity are emphasized in personal inquiries. Subjective experiences, personal perceptions of selfhood, and interconnectedness with others and the world are highlighted, questioning the human condition, identity, and meanings of life. To get started one might ask questions such as: What is my role, purpose, responsibility regarding this issue/problem? Who do I think I am as an educator and human being? How have I come to certain beliefs about education, teaching, students, etc.? What have my own lived experiences being educated and educating been like?

- **Critical inquiries:** Interrogating established structures of social, cultural, and political power are emphasized in critical inquiries. Shedding light upon taken-for-granted biases and ideological proclivities, critical inquiries strive to identity and contest various manifestations of oppression. To get started one might ask questions such as: What potential inequities are involved? How are concerns related to justice being addressed? How is power operating?

- **Communicative inquiries:** Viewpoint diversity and reciprocal dialogue are emphasized in communicative inquiry. The interactive co-construction of ideas and values through ongoing conversations is the basis for this form of inquiry. To get started one might ask questions such as: With whom am I (should I be) in dialogue? Who is affected by my curriculum decisions? What are my conversations with others like? What words, phrases, and other discourse are commonly used or not, and why?

- **Dialectical inquiries:** Exploration of contradictions is emphasized in dialectical inquiry. Understand how conflicting ideas, values, and beliefs change over time and shape the evolution of prevailing social, political, and cultural perspectives are outcomes of such inquiry. To get started one might ask questions such as: What persistent and potentially irresolvable tensions are involved? How often are educational matters discussed (and thought of) in terms of either/or dichotomies rather than both/and?

- **Ecological inquiries:** Oftentimes ecological inquiry is linked to science through the study of ecosystems and issues of environmental sustainability. While this is not wrong, ecological inquiries can be much broader. Ecological inquiries highlight relationships and connections and how nothing ever exists in a vacuum. Such inquiry explores the interconnectedness and interdependence between individuals, their communities, and the environment in shaping educational experiences and the context in which learning occurs. To get started one might ask questions such as: How am I nested within relationships such as cultural practices and social issues specific to an educational context? How am I participating in these, and how have/are these inhabiting me?

The aims of eclectic curriculum studies are fully educational. Eclectic professional study of this sort resists reducing professional education to mere endeavors of credentialing and training. Attending to the intellectual and moral dimensions of educational authority, these six forms of inquiry can support teachers' and school leaders' professional artistry. Professional artistry requires teachers' and school leaders' relative autonomy, as Biesta might argue, affording them a fair chance at being subjects of their own personal and professional lives. Table 5.1 distinguishes eclectic curriculum studies for professional artistry from professional credentialing and training processes. While credentialing and training programs can have value, eclectic curriculum studies for professional artistry attends to the intellectual and moral complexities of teaching. Table 5.1 contrasts the goals and approaches of credentialing and training with those of eclectic curriculum studies aimed at fostering professional artistry. While credentialing processes focus on standardized methods and outcomes, eclectic curriculum studies prioritize diverse, intellectually and morally rich forms of inquiry that support educators' professional autonomy and artistry.

Maintaining professional artistry and intelligent forms of compromise empowers teachers and school leaders to consider their individual platforms in relation to institutional norms. This holistically imagined platform, including one's own educational vision and other allied or competing visions, provides a basis for choosing how to act in their professional context. *Often, curriculum workers encounter significant discrepancies between their platform visions and their school's institutional priorities. However, there are many ways professional educators can respond to such discrepancies.* When

TABLE 5.1

Credentialing and Training	**Eclectic Curriculum Studies for Professional Artistry**
Instrumental techniques and strategies	Practical inquiry
Standardized achievement	Personal inquiry
Ideological distortion and rigid reasoning	Critical inquiry
Top-down directives	Communicative inquiry
Either/or thinking	Dialectical inquiry
Fragmented organizations and relationships	Ecological inquiry

professional artistry through practical and eclectic inquiry is sacrificed, teachers and school leaders tend to act in nonreflective or managed ways. In such cases, teachers might be controlled by a scripted program. They might even embrace this lack of autonomy because it relieves them from responsibilities related to exercising professional judgment. However, many, if not most, teachers are attuned to the moral dimensions of their work. They will find or even make wiggle room that affords them opportunities to exercise professional autonomy. Five approaches to curriculum discourse and action are highlighted in table 5.2.

Deciding how to proceed is a decision teachers and school leaders make about how to exercise their professional authority. If carried out with practical wisdom, it is a decision that requires a holistic imagination with what Freire (2018) called *conscientização*. Typically translated into English as *conscientization* and generally understood as the development of a critical awareness of one's social reality, *conscientização* is an ongoing process of interrogating dominant power structures, questioning prevailing assumptions, and understanding the ethical as well as the sociopolitical dimensions of curriculum and pedagogy. Broad awareness of the coexistence of multiple curricula (i.e., planned, actualized, received, explicit, implicit, null), and careful considerations of the key elements and orientations of curriculum practice bring the interconnectivity of curriculum discourse and action and pedagogical relations to the fore.

Table 5.2, which you should be familiar with from chapter 1, presents five approaches to curriculum discourse and action, each grounded in a distinct basis and set of actions. These approaches, ranging from nonreflective adherence to habits and customs to peace-oriented

TABLE 5.2

Five Approaches to Curriculum Discourse and Action

Approaches to Curriculum Discourse and Action	Basis	Actions
Nonreflective	Habits and customs	Following past precedent
Technical-managerial	Managed consensus building	Building efficient/effective and coherently designed plans
Deliberative	Consensus building through collegial conversations	Multi-perspective deliberation
Conflict-oriented	Ethical and political responsibilities	Resistance, opposition, noncompliance
Peace-oriented	Nonviolence, interconnectivity, and interdependence	Noncoercive action, action without force, noninstrumental engagement, transforming inner and outer relationships, civil resistance and disobedience

engagement in noncoercive actions, reflect the diverse ways educators might exercise professional authority. The approaches provide educators with multiple options for reflecting on their actions with their values in educational contexts. Moreover, each approach offers a different pathway for engaging with Freire's concept of *conscientização*—the development of critical awareness and a deep understanding of the ethical and sociopolitical dimensions of education.

Teaching Implications

Eclectic curriculum studies and tactful teaching go hand in hand. Teachers exercise their professional authority in ways that affect what is being conveyed in their classrooms and how educational content is presented to their students. When appreciating the intimate relationship between curricular and pedagogical decisions, it is essential not to conflate these two facets of educational practice. Curriculum is everything that is conveyed in an educational situation. It involves numerous decisions about how to represent the natural and cultural world in educational situations, and it is concretized through the organization of educational content and purposes. Pedagogy is a relational phenomenon involving teachers, students, and curricula. Pedagogical decisions are judgments about how to approach presenting representations of nature and culture (i.e., curricula) to students. Pedagogical artistry is also about finding tactful ways to address irresolvable tensions within educational situations, appreciating that pedagogical issues are not problems to resolve but relationships to nurture continuously.

This book's emphasis on engaging curriculum theory recognizes that curriculum and pedagogy are distinct but entangled elements of education and aims to underscore teachers' vitally important role as curriculum workers. Teachers make countless decisions about how the world is represented and presented to their students, even in the most controlled professional contexts. As one responds to the institutional norms, theoretical character, and conditions of curriculum practice that shape how the world is represented in educational situations, teachers also must consider how the curricula are presented to their students through pedagogical relationships. Friesen and Su (2023) describe a variety of tensions teachers negotiate within pedagogical situations. Consider how teachers exercise professional judgment related to the five irresolvable tensions.

- **The first tension is between the child's present and their future.** To some extent, teaching is always a forward-looking enterprise. Teachers rightfully want to prepare their students for their anticipated futures. However, educational discourse in the United States has taken its focus on students' anticipated futures to a potentially dangerous extreme. The discourse of readiness permeates all levels of education. Teachers are expected to promise college and career readiness in high schools. In preschools, the dominant aim is Kindergarten readiness. Even university-based teacher educators are expected to verify their graduates are ready for the classroom. Educators are ceaselessly pressured to pursue readiness even though consensus on what readiness means is perennially elusive (Graue, 1993). Yet concern for the future needs to be tactfully balanced with considerations of the child's needs in the here and now. As Friedrich Schleiermacher argued at the onset of modern education, one should not sacrifice the child's present for their future.

- **The second tension is between teachers' responsibilities to protect students and their responsibility to expose them to new horizons of experience.** A curriculum is a particular way of organizing educational purposes and content, and it represents the natural and cultural world. However, representations of the world are not the real world. Instead, a curriculum comprises the aspects of the world that educational authorities have decided students should be exposed to. While making decisions about the official or planned curricula, teachers also make important choices about the null curriculum, elements of the nature and culture that are not reflected in the curriculum. Null curricula can include important but overlooked content that has unintentionally been omitted from the official curriculum. However, the intentional dimension of null curricula includes content deemed less critical that has been deliberately omitted and facets of the world that educational authorities have decided students should be protected from during their educational experience.

- **The third tension is between the teachers' (or other curriculum decision makers') proximity and distance to the child.** Consider how teachers choose to physically position themselves in their classrooms. Working on a task hand-over-hand or a young child sitting in a caregiver's lap are examples of extreme proximity a teacher might have to a child. An example of an incredibly distal relationship is curriculum developers creating a scripted program for children they have never met and will not meet in the future. Pedagogically, most teacher-student interactions are somewhere between these two extremes. How distal or how proximal teachers choose to be to their students is a matter of ongoing situational judgment.

- **The fourth tension is creating atmospheres that nourish freedom while upholding necessary constraints.** There are perennial tensions between freedom and constraint in classrooms. On the one hand, most educators acknowledge the value of allowing some level of student autonomy. On the other hand, few educators want their classroom to become an "anything goes" environment. Therefore, teachers are perpetually balancing freedom and constraints in pedagogical situations.

- **Lastly, the fifth tension is between individuality and commonality.** Few professional educators are responsible for only one student. Even if they are, educators have dual responsibilities to the child and the world. Therefore, they constantly balance considerations of individualized needs with the collective needs of the class, the school, or the larger community. As with the other dichotomies, the tension between individuality and community needs to be judiciously decided situationally.

Assessment Implications

It is imperative to continuously assess the outcomes of one's curriculum study and teaching activities. Ralph Tyler argued that a planning cycle is incomplete without intentional forms of assessment and evaluation. For Tyler, evaluation is a basic principle of curriculum and instruction, as are the determination of educational purposes and the selection and organization of learning experience. From an instrumental point of view, he raised the question (1949,104): "How can the effectiveness of learning experiences be evaluated?" However, Tyler's conception of evaluation focuses on the extent to which educational experiences change individuals according to purposes defined by predetermined learning objectives. It is important to consider evaluation as more than merely a measure of alignment with predetermined objectives. A broader view of assessment and evaluation encourages educators to examine the underlying educational purposes and values embedded within the curriculum.

Tyler's perspective on assessment and evaluation is ubiquitous in contemporary educational settings, and on the surface, it seems somewhat comprehensive. Though predetermined, objectives are derived from multiple sources: studies of learners, studies of contemporary life, and suggestions from subject area specialists. Moreover, by situating evaluation within the curriculum development process, Tyler's approach to evaluation is quite pragmatic, seeing it as "a process for finding out how far the learning experiences as developed and organized are actually producing the desired results" (105). Knowing the strengths and limitations of one's practice enables teachers and school leaders to make well-informed curricular and pedagogical adjustments.

At first glance, Tyler's insistence on assessing students on multiple occasions rather than at a singular moment may assuage many concerns about high-stakes standardized testing. However, a closer look reveals that Tyler's broad-minded instrumentality imposes comprehensive control mechanisms upon practice through evaluation. Educators are frequently obligated to show evidence of measurable student outcomes and monitor students' progress on an ongoing basis. The premise that educational experiences should change a person in some predetermined way limits curricular practices to accrediting and socializing aims. Subjectification is much more challenging to measure and cannot be predetermined.

In this sense, the authority exercised in predetermining the ends of education is commonly concealed by the complex bureaucratic machinery. Evaluation is never ethically or politically neutral. Whose values are validated in the processes of assessment and evaluation? What assumptions about knowledge and learning underlie the chosen methods of assessment and evaluation? How do the pressures for measurable outcomes influence the kinds of learning experiences that get prioritized? For Tyler, such questions are resolved by a philosophical screen, and if he were alive, he would likely lament that our contemporary discourse and educational institutions inadequately reflect a democratic orientation. He identified four values of democratic philosophies of education:

The recognition of the importance of every individual human being as a human being regardless of his race, national, social, or economic status; (2) opportunity for wide participation in all phases of activities in the social groups in the society; (3) encouragement of variability rather than demanding a single type of personality; (4) faith in intelligence as a method of dealing with important problems rather than depending upon the authority of an autocratic or aristocratic group. (1949, 34)

More recently, Susan Neiman (2023) echoed a commitment to these democratic values in her defense of liberal values derived from the modern European enlightenment. Yet, Neiman's contemporary perspective takes a decisively more defensive tone than Tyler's statement, which is now over seventy-five years old. In the middle of the twentieth century, progressive educators like Tyler presumed curriculum workers would commonly embrace philosophies of education that emphasize democratic values. Neiman, a contemporary philosopher, is not nearly as presumptuous. She argues against what she perceives to be three common philosophical threats to democratic ways of life: tribalism, the conflation of justice and power, and discourse that renders progress impossible. In this sense, her assertions that universal truths and values exist, power does not equal justice, and that progress is possible are articulated against an image of authoritarianism.

Assessing student outcomes for democratic good living builds upon Tyler's insights that evaluation should be ongoing and holistic. Holistic 3S educational outcomes encompass students' **subject** matter understanding in ways that are useful to understanding **oneself** and one's society. However, assessing student outcomes against authoritarianism rejects polarizing politicization, unaccountable uses of power, and doomsday pessimism. It accounts for positive and negative educational side effects, which curriculum theorists have explored with concepts like hidden and null curricula. In other words, anti-authoritarian assessment is open to possibilities for unanticipated outcomes, appreciating the potential harm of trying to predict and control every aspect of educational experiences. Unanticipated educational outcomes can be either positive or negative. When educational authorities share power and control, they are not guaranteeing beneficial results. Still, they are expanding appraisals of holistic 3S educational outcomes to consider if and how students are becoming subjects of their own lives.

Implications for Reflection

Curriculum studies and reflective practices bookend the STAR activities, highlighting two vital professional development pathways. Through eclectic study and multimodal reflection, professional educators grow, learn, and develop as curriculum workers. Too often, reflective teaching is reduced to technical questions: Did the curricular or pedagogical decisions work? What adjustments could be made to improve the effectiveness and efficiency of our practices? While these are obviously important questions, technical reflection only addresses curriculum and pedagogy at the surface level. Mirroring the interdisciplinarity and philosophical diversity of curriculum studies, a field prominently understood as an extraordinarily complicated conversation (Pinar et al., 1995), reflective practitioners reflect in and on action. Further, like eclectic curriculum studies, multi-modal reflective practices interrogate the intellectual and moral complexities of curriculum and teaching. To support experiential learning, we link eclectic curriculum studies to five modes of reflective inquiry.

Practical inquiries correspond to *techne* and *phronesis*, or **technical reflection** and **practical wisdom**. Teachers reflect upon the instructional strategies they employ. Technical reflection involves the consideration of instrumental decisions in planning and carrying out instruction and assessments. Did the selected strategy or framework work to the teachers' satisfaction? Are there ways instruction could be made more effective or efficient by selecting an alternative approach to lesson design or reorganizing an instructional unit? Did students demonstrate understanding of the key ideas or concepts? Teachers use practical wisdom when they reconsider their practices concerning the particularities of people, contexts, and situations at hand. Good teaching is an ongoing exercise in using sound, practical judgment. What is best for these students, in this place, at this time, in this situation?

Personal inquiries correspond to *poesis*, or **personal introspection**. Personal introspection is an important dimension of reflective practice. Education is a deeply personal journey of understanding. Who am I as an educator? What is it I do? Am I happy with myself, who I am, and who I am becoming personally and professionally? How do my personal experiences and identity shape the way I approach my students and the curriculum? Am I living in a way that reflects my deepest values, or are there areas where I feel out of alignment? What personal habits or thought patterns are helping or hindering my growth as an educator? What role does self-compassion play in my professional journey, especially during challenging times?

Critical inquiries correspond to *praxis* and *polis*, or **sociopolitical reflection**. Schools are social institutions and education is inherently political. Sociopolitical reflection brings these often implicit dimensions of teaching to the fore with critical examinations of whose needs and interests are addressed in educational situations and whose are not. How can I best advocate for my students? How does curriculum as an institution work for and/or against their individual and collective interests? In what ways does the curriculum reinforce or challenge existing social inequalities? What policies or practices within the school contribute to equity and/or inequity? How do school policies on discipline, attendance, or grading reflect broader social values, and what impacts do they have on marginalized students? How does the broader sociopolitical context (e.g., local, national, or global events) impact my students' perspectives and learning needs?

Communicative inquiries correspond to *dialogos*, or **multi-perspective reflection**. Teaching is a relational practice. Educators should continuously reflect on their relationships to the natural and cultural world and varied interpretations of the world, while also carefully considering how to present themselves and the world to their students. How can/should a teacher simultaneously cultivate and maintain meaningful relationships with their students and their world? How can a teacher encourage students to engage with perspectives that differ from their own in constructive and compassionate ways? What practices help teachers (and others) to stay present and attentive to the needs, emotions, and perspectives of each student during interactions? How might deep listening be engaged in conversations? How can educators remain open to learning from students' unique insights and experiences? What factors might contribute to the communication breakdown? Was it related to content, misunderstandings, egoic projections or responses, and/or cultural differences?

Dialectical and ecological inquiries correspond to *theoria*, or **theoretical reflection**. Professional educators are curriculum theorists, even if they do not identify as such. As Walker reminds us, curriculum and scientific theories are very different. Scientists use logic and evidence to accept or reject theoretical propositions dispassionately. However, theories of education in general and curriculum in particular are more suitably grounded in humanities-based disciplines that "employ reason and evidence, but in the service of passion. . . . Curriculum theories make ideals explicit, clarify them, work out their consequences for curriculum practice, compare them to other ideals, and justify or criticize them" (2003, 60). What are the relationships among various facets of curriculum practice? How does one balance the irresolvable tensions of practice? What are the potential limitations and risks of a curriculum theory that overly prioritizes one educational ideal over others? What assumptions about human growth and learning underpin different curriculum theories, and how do these assumptions shape educational goals and experiences?

HI-STAR as an Intergenerational Conversation

In this section, we explore how curriculum and teaching draw from the past, respond to the present, and inspire action for the future. William Pinar (2007) describes this as the "verticality" and "horizontality" of the field of curriculum studies. Verticality represents the foundation—the accumulated wisdom and intellectual histories we build on. Horizontality is the here and now—the current challenges and context we engage with every day. But often something more is required—a dimension that connects past insights and present realities to ethical reflection and action. Henderson and Kesson (2009) call this *diagonality*: the dynamic, personal growth that happens when we weave together what we know from the past, what we face today, and the vision of what we strive for. In chapter 6, Jim narrates the verticality of the HI-STAR, showing how it was shaped by years of curriculum work. Then, in chapter 7, Jen and Dan build on that foundation and adapt it for today's classrooms with a commitment to meaningful and democratic teaching.

6

A Curriculum Legacy

Jim's Reflections on the HI-STAR Growth Process

This chapter presents my background story on how this book's approach to educators' moral-intellectual development through the practice of a HI-STAR growth process was gradually conceived over fifty-six years of curriculum and teaching studies. During this 1968–2024 time period, my focus was on continuously improving my understanding of the vital relationship between *democratic governance* and *democratic education*. In short, I wanted to address an important undertheorized professional development topic. My many years of collaboratively working on this research problem with visionary scholars and dedicated practitioners has resulted in the identification of *four ethical principles* as guides for educators' professional growth. Each principle addresses an important moral-intellectual "capability" (Nussbaum, 2011) for the arts of democratic teaching—for the cultivation of the necessary study, practice, assessment, and reflection capacities. Our book is a multifaceted developmental approach that addresses John Dewey's key point that, "with respect to the aims of education, no separation can be made between impersonal abstract principles of logic and moral qualities of character. What is needed is to weave them into unity" ([1910]1933, 34).

Our text's focus on a particular way to address this logical-moral interaction is inspired by the democratic public service of two great American presidents: George Washington and Abraham Lincoln. Washington's dedicated life as a revolutionary hero, constitutional delegate, and first US president provided inspirational leadership for the birth of America's democratic union, while Lincoln's inspired wartime leadership saved this union from dissolving due to a contentious, unprincipled practice of human slavery.

Both American presidents embody the personal pursuit of ethical excellence that is celebrated by the French philosopher Luc Ferry, an academic philosopher who also served as the National Minister of Education for his country's government. Ferry's book, *Homo Aestheticus: The Invention of Taste in the Democratic Age*, is a sophisticated argument for a deep personal embrace of democratic integrity through the practice of a "judicial humanism [which] holds that my freedom ends there where the other person's freedom begins" (1993, 258–59). He views the cultivation of this ethical integrity as critically important for our interdependent, pluralistic world; and Doris Kearns Goodwin's biography of Lincoln vividly captures the spirit of Ferry's aesthetic argument. Goodwin concludes her historical narrative of Lincoln's democratic presidential leadership in this way:

His conviction that we are one nation, indivisible, "conceived in Liberty, and dedicated to the proposition that all men are created equal," led to the rebirth of a union free of slavery. And he expressed this conviction in a language of enduring clarity and beauty, exhibiting a literary genius to match his political genius. With his death, Abraham Lincoln had come to seem the embodiment of his own words—"With malice toward none; with charity for all"—voiced in his second inaugural to lay out the visionary pathway to a reconstructed union.

(2005, 749)

Going back in time to George Washington's democratic public service, he was not perfect. He did own slaves; but despite this critical ethical flaw, he serves as an inspirational model for twenty-first-century educators around the world who see themselves as visionary advocates and servants of their country's democratic aspirations. Two personal moments in Washington's career highlight the personal aesthetic depth of his leadership: his voluntary retirement as the commanding revolutionary general in 1783 and his voluntary retirement as the United States' first president in 1797. Both of these signature events were powerful public demonstrations of the peaceful transfer of power, which is an essential feature of constitutional democracies. Washington's 1796 *Farewell Address* includes this ethical advice:

The alternate domination of one faction over another, sharpened by the spirit of revenge, natural to party dissension, which in different ages and countries has perpetrated the most horrid enormities, is itself a frightful despotism. . . . It is of infinite moment, that you should properly estimate the immense value of your national Union to your collective and individual happiness; that you should cherish a cordial, habitual, and immovable attachment to . . . the *sacred ties* which now link together the various parts.

A key feature of Washington's public service to the promise of American democracy was his political leadership in the creation of the US constitution, which was formerly approved in 1787. This document, which is the most enduring democratic constitution in human history, can be described as a sacred national document guided by a set of constitutional assertions and doctrines addressing the establishment, maintenance, and continuous improvement of democratic governance: a universal rule of law; the practice of fair elections and equal legal protection; the balance of power between executive, legislative, and judicial powers; and the enactment of an amendable bill of rights. With reference to this constitutional design, it can be argued that Lincoln's most important public service to American democracy was his patient, determined efforts to secure the passage of the Thirteenth Amendment to the US constitution, which legally abolished slavery. This amendment was formally ratified in December 1865, which was eight months after his assassination.

Unfortunately, neither President Washington nor President Lincoln clarified and promoted the necessary educational policies and practices that addressed the continuous growth of American citizens' democratic values. In short, this vital feature of a thriving democracy was left unattended. On the eve of the United States' entrance into the Second World War, Dewey ([1939] 1989) noted the cultural consequences of this instructional inattention: "We [Americans] have advanced far enough to say that democracy is a way of life. We have yet to realize that it is a way of *personal life* and one which provides a moral standard for *personal conduct*" (101). Dewey is highlighting the cultural consequences of what—in curriculum studies terminology is called a "null curriculum problem." Eisner explains this type of educational inattention:

> It is my thesis that what schools do not teach may be as important as what they do teach. Ignorance is not simply a neutral void; it has important effects on the kinds of options one is able to consider, the alternative that one can examine, and the perspectives from which one can view a situation or problem. . . . A parochial perspective or simplistic analysis is the inevitable progeny of ignorance.
>
> (1994a, 158)

Perhaps the null curriculum problem that Dewey is addressing is due to the fact that America's eighteenth- and nineteenth-century political leaders did not have a deep understanding of the vital relationship between the constitutional legalities of democratic governance and the ethical dispositions of democratic living. Perhaps, if John Dewey had been a contemporary of these politicians, they would have been more dutifully mindful of this critical legal-personal interaction. In his *My Pedagogic Creed*, Dewey ([1897] 2017, 39–40) writes:

> The community's duty to education is . . . its paramount moral duty. . . . Education thus conceived marks the most perfect and intimate union of science and art conceivable in human experience. The art of thus giving shape to human powers and adapting them to social service is the supreme art; one calling into its service the best of artists; that no insight, sympathy, tact, executive power, is too great for such a service.

The founders of Finland's democratic constitution, which was finalized in 1919, did understand the importance of practicing the pedagogical artistry that Dewey advanced in 1897 and throughout his academic career. As a result, their teacher education programs and public schools are consistently rated as the best in the world. I was the keynote speaker for Finland's first national Teacher Leader Conference, which was held at the University of Helsinki in May 2013. My speech addressed the topic of "Teacher Leadership for a Visionary Democratic Education." Working with Dewey's conception of pedagogical artistry, I presented a way that Finnish teacher leaders could advance their country's democratic aspirations through a study-based, collegial professional development. This book's HI-STAR growth process is a refinement of this 2013 speech; and given the history of Finland's policy support for public education, it's not surprising that my keynote address was enthusiastically received. Following the conclusion of my presentation, I conducted a question-and-answer forum with the Finnish teacher leaders. One of the educators asked me, "Why don't Americans carefully study and practice the advice of John Dewey, who is their greatest educational philosopher?" As you can imagine, I did not have an answer to her question.

I now turn to the presentation of my 1968–2024 scholarship, which informs the design of this book. My narrative is organized into *six curriculum study themes*. Before turning to my story, I want to conclude this introductory section by respectfully acknowledging the contemporary American educators I have met over the years who intuitively embrace the professional growth we are formally conceptualizing and advancing in this text. My narrative would not be complete without honoring them. Though they had not been formally introduced to the disciplined professional growth in this book, they already had an underlying feel for the historic importance of linking democratic living and educational artistry.

Theme 1: Studying Liberalizing Transformative Education

In 1968, after completing my BA liberal arts degree in history at Dartmouth College, I immediately enrolled in an innovative and accelerated, two-year "Teacher Intern" master's degree program at the University of Wisconsin–

Milwaukee (UWM). As a policy response to the critical teacher shortage in Wisconsin, this creative graduate program combined preservice professional development with academic educational studies. I chose to balance my teacher education curriculum with a disciplined examination of the cultural and philosophical foundations of American education. My first foundations course in the summer of 1968 was an educational philosophy seminar taught by Dr. Normand Bernier. One of the assigned texts in his seminar was John Dewey's *Individualism Old and New.* In this concise essay, Dewey ([1930] 1984) calls for the cultivation of an "integrated individuality" through liberalizing educational experiences grounded in present-day problem-solving. He writes:

> Individuality is at first spontaneous and unshaped; it is a potentiality, a capacity of development. . . . To gain an *integrated individuality*, each of us needs to cultivate his/her own garden. But there is no fence about this garden: it is no sharply marked-off enclosure. Our garden is the world, in the angle at which it touches our own manner of being. By accepting the . . . world in which we live, and thus by fulfilling the pre-condition for interaction with it, we, who are also parts of the moving present, create ourselves as we create an unknown future.
>
> (81–83)

I felt that Dewey's argument was a confirmation of my undergraduate education that concluded with an honors thesis project addressing George Washington's revolutionary leadership. My thesis advisor was Crane Brinton, the internationally respected author of *The Anatomy of Revolution* (1965). I felt that Dewey was discussing the liberalizing undergraduate education I had just received, which is insightfully explained by the Baylor University curriculum scholar Wesley Null:

> Forgotten to many people today, the term *liberal* in liberal education has nothing to do with politics or left-leaning views on hot-button issues. Liberal education, rather, refers to an interdisciplinary approach to curriculum and teaching that pursues the goal of liberating minds so that they become more fully human, make rational judgments, and provide civic leadership.
>
> (2017, 15)

As I studied Dewey's *Individualism Old and New,* I felt excited about pursuing my personal growth as a new teacher with his understanding of American individualism as an ethical guide. I understood the dialectical challenges of this professional development. My liberal arts studies at Dartmouth were equally exciting and disturbing since much of my religious and socio-emotional upbringing was challenged. However, as a swimming and track athlete in high school and college, and as an age-group swimming coach at the onset of my teaching career, I recognize that, "there is no gain without pain." To this day, I feel extremely grateful for the broadening of my personal horizons that occurred during my undergraduate education.

Both John Dewey and the influential nineteenth-century German educational philosopher Johann F. Herbart understood the dialectical challenges of liberalizing, integrating educational experiences. The contemporary American philosopher, Andrea English, describes these challenges as the inevitable "discontinuities" in transformative education, and her book provides an astute, comparative analysis of Herbart's and Dewey's understanding of democratic teaching dialectics. I strongly recommend that readers of our book carefully study her text. It's filled with important insights into the professional growth process we are advancing. English summarizes her comparative analysis of Herbart's and Dewey's educational philosophies as follows:

> Teaching is increasingly construed as transmitting predetermined outcomes to students and then using standardized testing to verify that students have achieved these outcomes. . . . The danger is that teachers may entirely overlook the educative value of difficulty and doubt, that is, of forms of discontinuity and negativity in experience and learning. . . . In Chapter 2, I address Herbart's two-part theory of education by examining his notions of the teacher's task as both supporting the learner's expansion of horizons through "educative instruction" and providing "moral guidance," respectively. . . . In Chapter 4, I analyze Dewey's concept of teaching and argue for an understanding of teaching as "teaching in-between." I argue that, for Dewey, reflective teaching provokes learners to dwell in the realm *between* right and wrong answers.
> (2013, xxii–xxv)

Our creation of the HI-STAR growth process is guided by this vision of teachers cultivating their moral-intellectual capacities to teach for the democratic liberalizing of their students' personal horizons. This is why the acronym for our professional development approach begins with an *HI*, referring to working with a holistic, imaginative curriculum platform. Educators with this foundational orientation are careful to not confuse the parts with the whole—a narrow conception of student achievement instead of a big-picture understanding of educational excellence. Such teachers don't get caught up in confining pedagogical ideologies. They approach their pedagogy work with a "beyond belief" frame of reference that embraces Socratic doubt and diverse ideological perspectives (Bernier and Williams 1973). In short, their educational engagements with their students, their colleagues, and all other relevant curriculum stakeholders are holistically imaginative.

The growth of this liberalizing individualism can occur in many ways—through personal relationships, domestic and foreign travels, challenging hobbies, and so on. Abraham Lincoln did not have access to a formal liberal arts education; however, he made a point of cultivating his personal horizons through late-night, candle-lit reading in his humble log cabin (Goodwin, 2005). The six inquiry pathways in our HI-STAR growth process are designed to cultivate such liberalizing breadth so that educators are well positioned to embody and teach democratic goodness.

Theme 2: Studying Critical, Contemplative, and Loving Integration

My summer 1968 educational philosophy seminar with Dr. Bernier ended with two final-exam options: take a two-hour written exam in the university classroom or participate in a weekend retreat at a farm north of Milwaukee. Most of the students in the course chose the writing option, but four of us chose the second option, which was described as a first-time, experimental Socratic dialogue on the philosophical foundations of American education. Our curricular experiment actually lasted for a continuous four days—from Friday night to Tuesday afternoon without much sleep. Two additional UWM faculty members joined this Socratic undertaking: Dr. Bernice Wolfson, who was the author of influential publications on humanistic, individualized learning, and Dr. James Macdonald, who was the national leader of a critical, holistic "reconceptualization" of curriculum studies that had been initiated at the Association for Supervision and Curriculum Development's annual conferences in the mid-1960s. I was so deeply inspired by this four-day Socratic experiment that I asked Dr. Bernier to serve as my academic advisor; and during the 1968–1969 academic year, I enrolled in two additional educational foundations courses taught by Drs. Bernier and Wolfson and a study tutorial facilitated by Dr. Macdonald.

My independent study with Dr. Macdonald is particularly relevant to this second study theme. In his signature publication on reconceptualizing curriculum development, Macdonald argues for educational theorizing that extends beyond the work of two current professional groups: academic researchers who quantify learning and educational administrators who standardize teaching. He argued for the emergence of a third group of scholars who would inquire in a broadly liberalizing, humanizing educational artistry:

A third group of individuals look upon the task of theorizing as a creative intellectual task. . . . The purpose of these persons is to develop and criticize conceptual schema in the hope that new ways of talking about curriculum, which may in the future be far more fruitful than present orientations, will be forthcoming. At the present time, they would maintain that a much more playful, free-floating process is called for by the state of the [curriculum theorizing] art. . . . There is an article of faith involved which is analogous to Dewey's comment that educational philosophy was the essence of all philosophy because it was "*the study of how to have a world*." Curriculum theory in this light might be said to be the essence of educational theory because it is *the study of how to have a learning environment.*

([1971] 2000, 6, 12)

Macdonald's humanistic reconceptualizing leadership ultimately resulted in the establishment of a curriculum and teaching conference with its own journal. A signature feature of this conference, which became an annual October event at the Bergamo Retreat Center in Ohio, was Macdonald's balanced critical, contemplative approach to education:

The ancient Greeks distinguished between theory and practice as two ways of living: the contemplative and the political. I think this understanding holds for what I wish to present. The [critical] rationalist in curriculum theory is living a political way of life, explaining in order to affect the living context of education in a direct controlling way—a political action. I personally suggest that it is time to reaffirm the legitimacy of contemplative curriculum theory. . . . Let us accept meditative thinking on an equal footing with calculative thinking.

(Macdonald [1974] 1995, 173–74)

In his brief essay, *A Common Faith*, John Dewey touches on Macdonald's critical, meditative balancing with his examination of the inspired consciousness of good-hearted people who pursue a democratic way of life. Dewey (1934/1962, 79) celebrates their "passionate intelligence, as [an] ardor in behalf of light shining into the murky places of social existence . . . [a] *devotion*, so intense as to be religious." Ferry (2013, 171) describes this interpersonal devotion as the practice of a philosophy of love in which "feelings of fraternity and sympathy . . . are simply offshoots of the principle of love in the collective sphere." He then summarizes this devoted democratic philosophy with this entreaty: "Act in such a way that the maxim of your action can be universalized . . . not as a law of Nature, in [Immanuel] Kant's way, but as a law of Love."

Jim Macdonald embodied this loving way of educating, and it's unfortunate that he died so early in his illustrious career. Fortunately, Dr. William Pinar, who assumed the mantle of Macdonald's national leadership, continued along the same balanced, holistic path and ultimately accepted a

Canadian-sponsored endowed professorship at the University of Vancouver to internationally advance broad curriculum studies.

Theme 3: Studying Eclectic, Deliberative Educational Arts

I began my doctoral studies in Stanford University's "Curriculum and Teaching (C&T) Studies" program in 1974. My first graduate assistant responsibility was working on a national curriculum evaluation project led by Drs. Joseph Schwab, Elliot Eisner, and Decker Walker. This was a major undertaking, and I became a member of a team of five graduate assistants helping the three professors. Joe Schwab had just retired after a productive career as an influential curriculum studies scholar at the University of Chicago (UC). His signature academic work was on clarifying and advancing the integration of practical and eclectic artistry in education. Dr. Schwab had served as one of Elliot Eisner's doctoral advisors at UC, and Decker Walker was Dr. Eisner's first PhD advisee at Stanford. After Dr. Walker received his doctoral degree, he was asked to join Stanford's C&T faculty. Consequently, there was a very close collegial relationship between Drs. Schwab, Eisner, and Walker; my third curriculum study theme is an integration and application of their collective scholarship.

Walker's dissertation research and subsequent scholarship was an examination of Schwab's eclectic and practical artistry in "naturalistic" curriculum development projects. Walker's concept of "naturalistic" curriculum development refers to educational projects that are not forced to fit into standardized management blueprints. In a coauthored book composed thirty-eight years after his dissertation research, Walker describes how educators and curriculum development groups actually engage in the design process in practice:

> They . . . never stated objectives at all; and those that did generally did so near the end, as a way of expressing their purpose to teachers, rather than at the beginning, as the fundamental starting point of their work. Their starting point appeared to be a *set of beliefs and images* they shared—*beliefs* about the content; about the students, their needs, and how they learn; about schools, classrooms, and teaching; about the society and its needs; and *images* of good teaching: of good examples of content and method, and of good procedures to follow. They spent a great deal of time stating and refining these beliefs [and images], which comprised what Walker called their [naturalistic] platform.
>
> (Walker 1971; Walker and Soltis 2009, 62)

After explaining naturalistic curriculum development, Walker and Soltis (2009) contrast the practical and eclectic artistry embedded in this approach with the historically dominant curriculum development "rationale" created by Ralph Tyler, who was another influential University of Chicago curriculum scholar. In his signature book, Tyler (1949) argues that educators should teach precise behavioral objects guided by an explicit format of predetermined answers to four fundamental questions: what are their educational purposes, what educational experiences will achieve these purposes, how should these experiences be organized, and how should the learning be evaluated. Contrasting Tyler's behavioral engineering format with their naturalistic orientation, Walker and Soltis note that,

> Schwab's deliberative process of curriculum planning . . . brings to the foreground aspects of the process that are consigned to a minor place in Tyler's model—deliberation, judgment, focus on the particulars of the situation, the need for considering a variety of concepts and ideas. Schwab regards both means and ends as mutually determining one another, whereas Tyler insists that our actions, *means*, must be adjusted to our objectives, *ends*.
>
> (2009, 63)

Elliot Eisner applied Schwab's practical, eclectic artistry to a holistic conception of educational aims that guides creative teaching enlightened by arts-based criticism. In his scholarship, Eisner invites teachers to work with a balanced approach to behavioral, problem-solving, and expressive objectives. He argues that "when specific skills or competencies are appropriate . . . [behavioral] objectives can be formulated, but one should not feel compelled to abandon educational aims that cannot be reduced to measurable forms of predictable performance" (Eisner 1994a, 113). In his discussion of the vital importance of including problem-solving objectives and expressive learning outcomes in one's instructional repertoire, he writes:

> The use of problem-solving objectives places a premium on cognitive flexibility, on intellectual exploration, and on the higher mental processes . . . , [while] expressive outcomes are the consequences of curriculum activities that are intentionally planned to provide a fertile field for personal purposing and experience.
>
> (118–19)

Eisner then discusses how an expansive holistic approach to educational aims requires a teaching artistry that is nurtured and supported by educational criticism. He considers this to be such an important matter that he follows his chapter on the "art of teaching" (Eisner, 1994a) with five chapters on "reshaping assessment in education" through an informing qualitative criticism that functions like the instructive, enlightening insights of thoughtful critics working in a wide range of creative arts. Eisner further develops this artistry-evaluation integration in his *Cognition and Curriculum Reconsidered* (1994b) and *The Enlightened Eye: Qualitative Inquiry and the Enhancement of Educational Practice* (2017). Walker's and Eisner's interpretations of Schwab's practical and eclectic artistry in education serve as the blueprint for my third curriculum study theme. Our creation of the HI-STAR growth process is an inquiry-based application of their scholarship. The goal of our professional development format is to study and practice an eclectic, deliberative pedagogical artistry. I will have more to say about this in the conclusion of my personal narrative.

Theme 4: Studying Caring in Democratic Education

My work on this curriculum study theme began in a difficult but unexpectedly inspiring way. Working with my advisor, Dr. Eisner, and two additional Stanford faculty members, I completed an initial draft of my dissertation project in the summer of 1979. The overall goal of my research was the creation of an informed, enlightening educational criticism of a second-grade teacher's artistry on ways to integrate playful learning into schoolwork. This ingenious, innovative educator worked in the Menlo Park Public School District and had developed her work-play creativity over many years through the disciplined study of educational games. She lived in a two-bedroom apartment in Menlo Park, and one of her bedrooms was actually a well-organized library of more than one hundred instructive games.

I prepared my educational criticism of her teaching artistry in two ways. Through an in-depth literature study, I created a conceptual map of the diverse ways humans interpret work and play in their daily activities, and I spent hours observing how the second-grade teacher's work-play creativity fit within this map. In effect, I was building my capabilities to engage in a qualitative, enlightening evaluation of this teacher's pedagogical artistry. When she read my final educational criticism of her instructional approach, she found it to be complimentary, encouraging, and informing.

Though my *dissertation committee* confirmed that I had achieved my research goal, I still had to successfully defend my dissertation in front of a separate *defense committee* that would include my advisor, Dr. Eisner, and four new Stanford faculty members. One of these defense committee members was Dr. Nel Noddings, who had been recently hired as an assistant professor in Educational Philosophy. When I presented my initial dissertation draft to my defense committee, I was applauded for my comprehensive literature study on human work and play and for my careful empirical observations. However, there were serious questions about the reliability and validity of this research. In effect, I was being asked to defend the "objectivity" of my subjective educational criticism. I immediately recognized that I was dealing with a "paradigm shift" problem, as insightfully examined by Thomas Kuhn in *The Structure of Scientific Revolutions* (1962) and as informed by James Macdonald's work on curriculum reconceptualization. Simply stated, there was no quick, easy way for me to defend my educational criticism as empirically objective educational research; consequently, the committee decided to postpone my dissertation defense until I could mount a more acceptable empirical argument.

Since Dr. Eisner was leaving Stanford for a one-year sabbatical at a British university, he felt that I should ask Dr. Noddings to serve as my interim dissertation advisor while he was gone. In 1979, internet communication was still in its infancy and not yet reliable. She agreed, and my collaborations with Dr. Noddings began in the fall 1979 quarter and were, ultimately, academically productive and very rewarding. Dr. Noddings and I worked out a methodological strategy to back up my "subjective" educational criticism with a valid, rigorous ethnographic analysis. I did not find this to be a difficult challenge for two key reasons. As part of my UWM master's degree studies, I had taken an excellent graduate seminar in ethnography at Columbia University taught by the famous anthropologist, Dr. Margaret Mead. More importantly, I was on the receiving end of Noddings's ethic of care; and I will have more say about her professional ethics and how she worked with me in a moment. When Dr. Eisner returned to Stanford in the summer of 1980, I was able to successfully defend my dissertation. My defense committee, which was chaired by a leading quantitative researcher and the acting dean of Stanford's Graduate School of Education (Dr. Arthur Coladarci), unanimously agreed that I had presented an empirically valid and reliable account of the second-grade teacher's work-play artistry. To paraphrase James Macdonald, the committee felt that my dissertation research was a vivid empirical, ethnographic analysis of *how to have a holistic, imaginative work-play learning environment* in an elementary school setting (Henderson 1980).

Though this account of my dissertation defense touches on my first three curriculum study themes, my main purpose for sharing this dissertation drama is to present my personal experience with Dr. Noddings's ethic of caring, which provides the substantive underpinnings of my fourth curriculum study theme. Noddings (1984, 176) writes that when a caring "teacher asks a question in class and a student responds, she receives not just the response but the student. What [that student] . . . says matters, whether it's right or wrong, and she probes gently for clarification, interpretation, contribution." Noddings summarizes this educationally caring relationship as an exercise in the interplay of confirmation, dialogue, and cooperative practice. Caring teachers confirm their students when they "attribute the best possible motive consonant with reality to the cared-for" (193) and then back up these attributions through dialogical practice. She writes, "Confirmation, the loveliest of human functions, depends upon and interacts with dialogue and [attentive] practice. I cannot confirm a child unless I talk with him and engage in cooperative practice with him" (196).

This fruitful, productive interplay of supportive dialogue, inspirational confirmations, and collaborative engagement was precisely how Dr. Noddings worked with me as my interim dissertation advisor. In chapter 9 of her *Education and Democracy in the 21st Century*, which is titled "Educating the Whole Person," Noddings (2013, 118) summarizes her caring ethic as follows:

> When thinking of moral life, Buber (1965) said, we should start with neither the collective nor the individual but with the *relation*. This recognizes that we become individuals largely through the relations to which we belong and that the strength and nature of these relations will affect our allegiance to or rejection of collectives. Care ethics posits relation as ontologically basic and the caring relation as morally fundamental. Our attention is on the *relation*, not solely or principally on the moral agent.

With reference to my first curriculum study theme, it's crucial to note that Noddings's argument for the moral centrality of caring relations in education has important implications for transformative learning. Teacher's caring support of students' cognitive and/or emotional dissonance is a key feature of democratic education. Throughout her book, Andrea English notes that both Johann Herbart and John Dewey had a deep understanding of this critical feature of pedagogical artistry. They both recognized that students' moral and intellectual growth required empathetic teachers willing to support their students' personal struggles with "in-between learning." English (2013) writes:

> What could it mean to preserve the in-between of experience for education? By reading Herbart and Dewey, as well as contemporary theorists' thoughts on the educative meaning of experiences such as inner struggle, felt difficulty, resistance, doubt, disillusionment, and fear, I have sought to demonstrate why we *should* preserve the in-between of experience for education. . . . The significance of the in-between of learning is grasped when we begin to understand that, in learning processes, the space that opens up when one is interrupted—confronted by something new and unfamiliar—is an experimental space for one to learn about oneself (one's limits and capacities) and about the world. In this space, learners can gain a sense of their own perfectibility.

(152)

Noddings's caring ethic was only one dimension of her passionate commitment to democratic education—a commitment that was consistently manifested throughout her publications. In her update and celebration of Dewey's 1916 signature text, *Democracy and Education*, that I have just cited, Noddings (2013, 19) writes:

> Indoctrination—even in the name of a great good—too easily leads to domination, authoritarianism, and even totalitarianism. Dewey put his trust in the "method of intelligence" through dialogue, responsible experimentation, and the evaluation of current experience. Students should come to the conclusions embraced by [thoughtful] social revisionists or to well-argued alternatives. But a serious problem remains today: How will students come to rational, moral conclusions on serious social/political issues if we cannot even discuss them? This is a problem we still face in the 21st century. Perhaps we do not need an elaborate, detailed theory of democracy, replete with principles to guide every decision. Dewey's emphasis on free and extensive communication within and across groups gives us a good start. Perhaps we should accept his advice and build our theoretical position as we go.

I will share more of Noddings's explanation of democratic caring in my next curriculum study theme.

Theme 5: Studying Reflective Inquiry in Democratic Education

Upon receiving my Stanford doctoral degree, I accepted an assistant professor position at Roosevelt University (RU) in Chicago, which I began in the 1980 fall semester. I was familiar with this university for two reasons. Elliot Eisner had received his undergraduate degree in art education from RU, and the university was an important part of the history of advancing democracy in American education. RU was established right after the Second World War as a conscious, proactive rejection of anti-Semitism in higher education. Affirming and celebrating this critical educational purpose, Eleanor Roosevelt—the widow of President Franklin Roosevelt—gave the keynote speech at RU's inaugural event in which she explicitly honored and applauded the university's commitment to the "enlightenment of the human spirit."

My main purpose for accepting employment at Roosevelt University was to gain practical professional development experience on the important interdependence between teacher education, curriculum studies, and educational leadership. As a new assistant professor, my responsibilities included teaching a *general teaching methods* course for undergraduates and a *fundamentals of curriculum* seminar for graduate students. I also served as a supervisor of student teachers in the Chicago Public Schools (CPS), as a teacher in RU's after-school social studies program for CPS students, and as a faculty collaborator in the creation of an EdD in *Interdisciplinary Leadership* for educators. In 1986, I was tenured and promoted to associate professor at RU and awarded a spring semester research leave to begin working with Elliot Eisner, Nel Noddings, and other curriculum theorists on my first book. My goal was to create a collaborative text that would provide guidance for practicing inquiry-based reflective teaching informed by the first four curriculum study themes I have just introduced.

This was a challenging book project that ultimately took me six years to complete. The first edition of *Reflective Teaching: Becoming an Inquiring Educator* was published in 1992. However, I was also quite preoccupied during this period with journal publications. Because I felt that I had now acquired sufficient practical experience with curriculum, teaching, and leadership interactions at RU, I was ready to seek employment at a university that would provide more research support and opportunities to work with Curriculum and Instruction (C&I) PhD students. To be an attractive candidate for such an academic position, I needed to increase my publication record. Fortunately, I successfully achieved my goal and was hired as an associate professor of curriculum studies at Kent State University (KSU) in 1990 to teach my RU *general teaching methods* and *fundamentals of curriculum* courses, as well as to create and teach a doctoral-level *curriculum theory* seminar and to provide organizational leadership for the College of Education's C&I PhD program and Professional Development School (PDS) network.

Though I was quite excited about this career change, I quickly recognized that I was facing a significant uphill professional challenge. With one exception, the KSU educational professors were curriculum specialists in Literacy Education, Mathematics Education, Middle School Education, Early Childhood Education, and other curriculum content fields. Though KSU's College of Education had an inclusive C&I PhD program that covered all content fields, certain colleagues wondered why an educator with a doctoral degree in general curriculum and teaching studies would have a tenured leadership position in their department.

Because I faced this professional skepticism at the onset of my KSU appointment, I knew that it would be quite important for me to clearly engage with the inspirational feature of this fifth curriculum study theme. I would need to quickly and consistently demonstrate that I could inspire undergraduate and graduate students—as well as the practicing teachers and administrators at our PDS sites—to embrace the elevated problem-solving that was my initial scholarship focus. Over my twenty-eight-year career at KSU, I successfully addressed this challenge, and I was pleasantly surprised in 2016 to be offered the College of Education's first-ever Endowed Chair in

Educational Leadership. When I retired in June 2018, a number of the C&I faculty personally thanked me for my work on inspiring and elevating their students' professional judgments.

I won't share a complete narrative of my academic and leadership activities from 1986 to 2018 on the topic of practicing an inspired, democratic reflective inquiry in education. During this thirty-two-year period, I published eleven collaborative texts that addressed different features of six interrelated topics: reflective inquiry in education, transformative curriculum leadership, instructional practical wisdom, curriculum and pedagogy integration, reconceptualizing curriculum development, and rethinking the Tyler rationale. However, I do want to share a few compelling episodes of my curriculum and teaching studies work during these years.

I'll begin with my many years of collaborating with a KSU colleague, Dr. Frank Ryan. Dr. Ryan is an academic philosopher advancing a contemporary "transactional" interpretation of John Dewey's final coauthored text, *Knowing and the Known* (Dewey and Bentley 1949). Over many years of lunchtime conversations, cooperative graduate advising, and collegial academic presentations, we discussed the evolution of Dewey's work on educational problem-solving beginning with his *How We Think: A Restatement of the Relation of Reflective Thinking to the Educative Process* (1909), and his *Logic: The Theory of Inquiry* (1938), that ultimately culminated with the 1949 coauthored *Knowing and the Known*.

Ryan (2011) summarizes this growth of Dewey's thinking in his essay titled *Seeing Together: Mind, Matter and the Experimental Outlook of John Dewey and Arthur F. Bentley*. In this short text, Ryan begins with a description of what he calls Dewey's "circuit of inquiry," which he summarizes in this way:

> *Logic: The Theory of Inquiry* was widely praised and largely neglected. . . . Perhaps the highlight of the *Logic* is the "pattern of inquiry," where Dewey . . . marks the onset of a problematic situation—an initial cognitive awareness that something is wrong and something needs to be done about it. When the answer is easy and readily available, the return to nonreflective thinking is quick and uneventful. But when the problem is obstinate, the solution not obvious, genuine inquiry is necessary. We need to devise a plan, idea, or hypothesis—first to diagnose the problem and then to decide how to resolve it. Dewey's circuit of inquiry . . . is an indispensable human asset, but . . . intellect does not operate in a vacuum. It requires physical instruments, tools, and data—often to diagnose a problem and formulate a hypothesis to resolve it, almost always putting the hypothesis to the test.
>
> (28–29)

Ryan then turns to Dewey's signature philosophical focus on advancing democratic "life transactions." He notes that this moral understanding of reflective inquiry turns Dewey's *circuit of inquiry* into a "circuit of valuation" where a value candidate is transformed into an authentic ethical enactment. He explains what occurs when engaged in a circuit of valuation:

> I must ask myself whether what I like, desire, or value *really* is likeable, desirable, or valuable. To determine this requires a test reflecting not just my present likes and dislikes, but the long-term interests of everyone affected by such an action, including myself. It requires, in other words, that a value candidate demonstrate its credentials as a genuine social value or good—not just a preference, but the end result of a process of valuation.
>
> (66)

Ryan then goes on to describe a dialectical contrast to circuits of valuation. This is empirical problem-solving where there is no integration between personal preferences and achievable goods. Such problem-solving is summarized as "transactional" in narrow, self-interested, narcissistic ways. For example, how many Americans today describe politicians they don't like as transactionally superficial con artists? Ryan then concludes by stating that without mindfully linking value candidates to enduring goods, the capacity to practice "authentic moral deliberation" is nonexistent. Dr. Ryan's concluding comments on circuits of valuation are quite pertinent to this fifth curriculum study theme. If current or prospective educators' developmental experiences with problem-solving topics are not grounded in compelling democratic ends-in-view, those activities are not addressing and cultivating the moral-intellectual development that is the ethical heartbeat of the HI-STAR growth process.

An excerpt from the foreword that Nel Noddings (1992) wrote for the first of my three editions of reflective inquiry in education nicely captures the overall blueprint of my collaborative publications between 1992 and 2018, which includes three editions of a follow-up transformative curriculum leadership book. In that foreword, Noddings writes:

> Three themes guide this fascinating and practical text: reflection, caring, and inquiry. . . . This text presents an unusually rich theoretical background for teachers. But theory is interwoven with a narrative that focuses on caring, commitment, and inquiry. . . . The authors encourage new and prospective teachers to learn about cooperative learning by engaging in it. Working together, they can practice collegial professional development and peer coaching. . . . The text also makes clear that caring in education is not just warm and cuddly feelings about students. It means commitment to continued inquiry and a steady devotion to modes of interaction that will bring out the best self in each student and in each teacher, too.
>
> (vii–viii)

Note Noddings's emphasis on the interrelationship of reflection, inquiry, and caring, on collegial collaboration, on continuing professional development, and on supportive transformative learning. As I pursued my KSU career, I published an additional five texts that were careful examinations of the interplay of the four topics that Noddings highlights in her foreword.

Two signature moments in my KSU teaching career provide some collegial insights into this fifth curriculum study theme. The first moment occurred in the undergraduate course Approaches to Teaching that I regularly taught from 1990 to 1993, and the second moment occurred in the graduate course Fundamentals of Curriculum that I regularly taught throughout my KSU tenure, from 1990 to 2018. I'm highlighting these two classroom episodes because they vividly capture the underlying spirit of all five study themes I have introduced.

The first episode occurred during one of my Approaches to Teaching classes. All three of my reflective inquiry editions included diverse reflections and inquiries that were expressed by four teacher characters: Johnny Jackson, who was an African American high school English teacher; Amy Nelson, a white elementary school teacher; Dennis Sage, a white kindergarten teacher; and Silvia Riveria, a Hispanic middle school teacher. Collectively, the four teacher characters represented the ideological camps in American education that are documented and discussed by Herbert Kliebard (2004) in his *The Struggle for the American Curriculum: 1893–1958*. Johnny's commentaries stressed critically informed reflections and inquiries on issues of social justice, while Amy addressed issues of professional competence. Dennis addressed issues of caring and contemplative wisdom, and Sylvia addressed the importance of multicultural mindfulness.

After introducing the professional beliefs to each teacher-character in positive ways, I encouraged students to think about how they might engage in constructive, naturalistic reflective inquiries with each of the four imaginary teachers. In effect, I was inviting my students, who would soon be practicing teachers, to "approach" their professional problem-solving in an ideologically eclectic spirit. Following my teacher-character introductions in one Approaches to Teaching course, a young tearful female student stopped to talk to me about the Dennis Sage character. She wanted to know the real-life teacher who modelled this spiritually contemplative character. I told her it wasn't just one individual instructor but a composite of teachers. She said that she had never met such an inspiring teacher, and I responded by inviting her to work on becoming such a caring, contemplative educator. She would then be proudly embodying the inspiration she's currently feeling for Dennis Sage. If I were talking with this undergraduate student today, I would conclude our conversation by inviting her to talk to Drs. Daniel Castner and Jen Schneider about their current teacher education work at Indiana University and Oklahoma State University. I would tell her that Dan and Jen are ethically powerful examples of the caring, contemplative Dennis Sage character that inspired her.

When I first met Dan at the 2007 American Association for the Advancement of Curriculum Studies (AAACS) conference in Chicago, he was thinking about applying to KSU's C&I PhD program. As we got to know one another, I felt that he was an embodiment of John Dewey's new individualism, Jim Macdonald's critical contemplation, and Nel Noddings's democratic caring; and I strongly encouraged Dan to begin his KSU doctoral curriculum studies as soon as he could. I first met Jennifer Schneider in my office during the fall 2009 semester. She was a new C&I PhD student who had just been assigned to be my graduate assistant. During our introductory conversation, I realized that, like Dan, she was also an intuitive embodiment of Dewey's, Macdonald's, and Noddings's professional ethics. I didn't share any of this to her; she was new to the curriculum study field, and I didn't want to overwhelm or scare her off. However, I happily realized that I had the opportunity to advise a doctoral student who had a strong intuitive feel for the educational ethics that I was conceptualizing.

As Dan's and Jen's doctoral advisor and collaborating scholar, it has been my joy to work with them on this text. Dan, Jen, and I began working on theorizing and designing the HI-STAR growth process in late 2018. We were joined by Dr. Thomas Kelly who, like me, had just retired in June 2018. He was a teacher educator at John Carroll University in University Heights, Ohio, for thirty-seven years. Over the years, Tom and I became close friends, and his assistance in creating this book has been invaluable. He didn't want to join us as a coauthor, but he was happy to help with the creation of this text.

The second signature moment that I want to highlight also requires some background information. At our first meeting in my office, I asked Jen if she would be interested in working with me as the lead author on the creation of an edited book celebrating the tenth anniversary of the Curriculum and Pedagogy (C&P) Group that had been initiated by James Sears and Louise Allen in 2000 (Henderson at al., 2010). Jen excitedly accepted my invitation, and she subsequently provided exemplary editorial leadership for this project. The text was published rather quickly and entitled, *The Path Less Taken: Immanent Critique in Curriculum and Pedagogy*. I asked Jen to compose a brief personal essay explaining her editorial duties for this text. She concludes her essay as follows:

> I have been introduced to the "complicated conversation" (Pinar, Reynolds, Slattery, and Taubman 1995) that surrounds curriculum studies. . . . I am not only beginning to make sense of curriculum studies' intellectual history and the foundational scholars in Jim's argument for immanent critique, but I am simultaneously gaining exposure to the field's present intellectual circumstance. To conclude, working on the

creation of [this text] has invited me to walk along the path less taken as presented in this book.

(Schneider 2010, 6)

A few years later at the American Educational Research Association's (AERA) 2012 annual meeting in Vancouver, I had a conversation with William Pinar on his argument that study should be the basis for all professional development activities in the field of education. Citing Robert McClintock's 1971 essay on the topic of disciplined study, Bill stated,

Study is the site of education. Not instruction, not learning, but study constitutes the process of education, a view, McClintock tells us, [that is] grounded in "individuality," "autonomy," and "creativity." McClintock . . . emphasizes the significance of our "particularity," that we become more than we have been influenced to be, that we . . . refashion ourselves by engaging "freely" and "creatively" with our circumstances.

(Pinar 2006, 112)

Pinar's position on this critical developmental topic was quite significant since, as I have mentioned earlier in this chapter, he had assumed the leadership of curriculum study reconceptualization after Jim Macdonald's early death. I told Bill that I was interested in creating a collaborative text that would illustrate his study-based developmental argument through highlighting the collegial study engagements of a doctoral-student team and a teacher-leader team. Bill liked the idea and decided that the book would be published in his Routledge "Studies in Curriculum Theory" series. The text was published in 2015 with the title, *Reconceptualizing Curriculum Development: Inspiring and Informing Action* (Henderson et al. 2015). All seven members of the doctoral-student team (Daniel Castner, Jennifer Schneider, Christine Fishman. Wendy Samford, Boni Wozolek, Beth Bilek-Golias, and Petra Pienkosky-Moran) worked together to compose personal chapters on their curriculum study topic; and the four-member teacher-leader team (Jen Griest, Jennifer Schneider, Susan School, and Konni Stagliano) worked together to compose a collaborative chapter titled "Lead-Learning Stories: A Narrative Montage." Schneider (2015) introduces their lead-learning montage in this way:

The concept of platform has been central for us developing and reflecting on the importance of this book's reconceptualization of curriculum development in relationship to our teaching. . . . The platform we present below is the result of our contemplations and personal, social transformations during the *TLEP* [KSU's *Teacher Leader Endorsement Program*] and through writing this chapter together. Our platform not only speaks to this book's vision for curriculum development but also to our concentrated efforts towards enacting more holistic visions in our schools, our classrooms, and our lives.

(143)

Routledge sent me extra copies of the published book, which I decided to give to my Fundamentals of Curriculum students in the fall 2015 semester. There were approximately twenty-five American and International master's and doctoral degree students in this graduate seminar, and I invited Jen, Jennifer, Susan, and Konni to be guest speakers on their chapter before I passed out the books. I told the four of them that they would have the entire 140 minutes of class time to present their collaborative "montage." As they started their collaborative talk, which involved much back-and-forth dialogue between the four of them, an amazing silence pervaded the classroom. I suddenly felt that I was sitting in a sacred space celebrating the power of pedagogical artistry. When Jen, Jennifer, Susan, and Konni concluded their montage presentation, the students gave them a rousing, standing ovation. It was a deeply moving moment and a powerful illustration of the moral-intellectual growth we are encouraging in this text.

Theme 6: Studying Dialectics in Democratic Education

As I share my own learning experiences with this curriculum study theme, I want to note that I could have easily presented this topic as the first instead of the last theme. Please keep in mind that, much like the four foundational guardrails of the US constitution, there's no particular order to these six study themes. All of them are equally important guides for cultivating the personal, professional growth we are advancing in this book.

I will introduce this sixth theme with a story that begins in 1997 when I began working with my good friend and colleague, Dr. Kathleen Kesson, on two educational projects. Kathleen had academic appointments in Curriculum and Teaching Studies at two institutions: Goddard College and the University of Vermont (UVM). One of her UVM responsibilities was to initiate a John Dewey Center at the university. Dewey was born and raised in Burlington, Vermont, and received his undergraduate degree at UVM. Kathleen informed me in early 1997 that she was planning an inaugural event for the John Dewey Center that would include a Friday evening New England Town Meeting on Dewey's life at his childhood home in Burlington followed by a Saturday evening keynote speech by Dr. Maxine Greene, who held the William F. Russell Endowed Chair on *Education and Freedom* at Teachers College, Columbia University. The selection of Dr. Greene as the keynote speaker was very appropriate due to her deep intellectual connection with John Dewey as a fellow Educational Philosopher. In fact, Dewey ended his illustrious academic career at Columbia University. In her *The Dialectic of Freedom* text, which I'll be shortly discussing in more detail, Greene (1988, xii) writes:

> This book began as a John Dewey Lecture and is presented with a sense of privilege evoked by the association with Dewey's name. Because Dewey himself so committed to intelligence and freedom, so ill at ease with the routine and unimaginative, I have no consciousness of being bound to an orthodoxy. The very thought of Dewey and the manner in which he "did" philosophy remain liberating, keeping me attuned to open possibility.

Kathleen Kesson invited me to attend the Friday evening Town Meeting and to introduce Dr. Greene at her Saturday evening keynote address. I enthusiastically thanked Kathleen for both invitations and felt honored and quite nervous about introducing such an important, influential educational philosopher. As I prepared my introductory speech, I felt it was quite important to celebrate Greene's understanding of democratic freedom:

> The growing, changing individual . . . always has to confront a certain weight in lived situations, if only the weight of memory and the past. There are ambiguities of various kinds, layers of determinateness. Freedom, like autonomy, is in many ways dependent on understanding these ambiguities, developing a kind of critical distance with respect to them. . . . When oppression or exploitation or segregation or neglect is perceived as "natural" or a "given," there is little stirring in the name of freedom. . . . When people cannot name alternatives, imagine a better state of things, share with others a project of change, they are likely to remain anchored or submerged, even as they proudly assert their autonomy.
>
> (Greene 1988, 9)

In these few sentences, Greene insightfully captures the essence of the passionate dialectical mindfulness that democratic educators need to develop so that they can constructively engage in the complex struggles between authentic democratic freedom and its contrary, opposing forces. I said this back in 1997 when I introduced Maxine, and I feel that this passionate mindfulness is even more important in 2024 due to the dramatic rise of right-wing authoritarian populism, anti-Semitism, and Christian nationalism in the United States and many other countries around the world.

In 1997, Kathleen Kesson and I also initiated a curriculum leadership project for a "Vermont Study Group" consisting of eight educational administrators and teachers. The members of this study group were engaged in a diverse assemblage of local curriculum leadership projects. With the assistance of one Australian and two American curriculum study scholars, we created a collegial study agenda on four dialectical topics: practicing naturalistic deliberation in managed schools, practicing democratic collaboration in standardized teaching systems, practicing critical dialogue in top-down educational hierarchies, and practicing poetic meaning-making in bureaucratized, disenchanted education.

When the Vermont curriculum leaders completed their studies, Kathleen and I asked one of the team members, Kerrin McCadden, to compose a reflective essay on her collegial experience. We also asked William Pinar to compose the foreword for this study-based project. Our edited book, *Understanding Democratic Curriculum Leadership*, was published in 1999. In his foreword, Dr. Pinar provides a succinct overview of the book's study-based dialectics:

> Henderson and Kesson have selected four critical topics . . . to be discussed by prominent curriculum scholars: (1) curriculum deliberation by Gail McCutcheon, (2) reflexive systems by Noel Gough, (3) cultural criticism by Joe Kinchcloe, and (4) educational mythopoetics by Kathleen Kesson. . . . It is quite clear that Henderson and Kesson appreciate the complexity of the current situation in the schools. They understand that democratic curriculum reform cannot proceed simply, as on a flowchart, as if procedural consensus could resolve [dialectical] political conflict.
>
> (viii)

Kathleen and I wanted Kerrin McCadden, who chairs her high school's English department, to have the final word in our edited text. McCadden's personal reflections are an honest and insightful examination of how teachers can constructively address the dialectical pressures they are facing. She concludes her essay with a vivid description of her semiprofessional constraints in dialectical tension with her professional leadership visions:

> The assumption that I have organized my teaching moments into quantifiable, concrete entities that might, assuming that they may be called to order, be sorted into compartments is a very loud "noise" in my world. Running down a rattling conveyor belt, my ideas of teaching *The Color Purple* (Walker 1982) are invoiced and listed on a packing slip as if they were stable things pulled from a shelf. How am I to resist homeostasis when my teaching is to be boxed? With recursive looping and reflexivity, we reject stasis. Telling "stories that never end" involves reading and subsequently rejecting part of all of that reading, never seeing the document the same way twice. We learn to "read" the document so it becomes generative. This word, "generative," threads its way through almost every idea in this [curriculum leadership] book. Even when we are being reminded to deconstruct, it is for the sake of continued change and growth. When we are asked to embrace conflict, conflict gives birth. When

we are brave enough to struggle for a mythopoetic curriculum, students and teachers can uncover untold awareness. It is vital to condition ourselves as educators to feel a cold shiver every time we begin to think we know any of the answers. This kind of comfort never inspired vision. (125–26)

McCadden's balanced critique raises an important dialectical matter in societies with democratic constitutions. America's constitutional, legal foundations for democratic governance are designed to promote and safeguard respectful pluralistic dialogue, not political obedience and conformity, and this is an important theme in George Washington's *Farewell Address* as highlighted earlier in this chapter.

Learning to practice fair-minded dialogue and deliberation in dialectical contexts by respectfully recognizing diverse perspectives, appreciating the nuances of complex matters, agreeing to disagree, practicing the arts of compromise, negotiating power relations, and so on—is a critical feature of generous and generative democratic living. I have already introduced Dr. Thomas Kelly, who was a teacher educator at John Carroll University. His assistance in creating this book has been invaluable; and in particular, Tom was an astute advocate of this sixth curriculum study theme based on his doctoral studies at the University of Wisconsin–Madison guided by Dr. Fred Newmann's curriculum and teaching scholarship. Throughout our biweekly work sessions on this book over many years, Tom and I would often refer to Newmann's seminal work on constructively addressing public controversies as a key ethical focus in practicing social justice (Newmann and Oliver 1970). See Kelly (1989, 2009, 2010, 2014) for a sample of how Newmann's influence was embedded throughout Tom's career as a teacher educator with a strong focus in civic education.

During our lengthy deliberations on the practice of democratic, dialectical mindfulness in education, Tom shared a summation of Newmann's work on an instructional model that is a vivid practical application of this sixth curriculum study theme. This teaching approach is titled the *Public Issues Model* and was a central feature of the Harvard Social Studies Project during the 1960s and 1970s. The model rests on the idea that citizens in a democracy differ in their views and priorities and that democratic values often conflict in specific cases. The resolution of complex public issues within democratic society requires citizens to negotiate their differences through careful analysis and public discussion. Helping students develop their abilities to take part in this conversation is thus a crucial aspect of democratic education. In the *Public Issues Model*, the purpose of discussion is not to resolve disagreements—although that can be an outcome—but to help students learn to state their ideas with more precision, to develop stronger rationales for their positions, and to understand precisely how their ideas are both similar to and different from those of others.

As a result of our lengthy discussions of the *Public Issues Model,* we created the following pedagogical guidance as a way of constructively addressing the three types of controversial issues conceptualized by Newmann. **Factual issues** arise when there is disagreement or uncertainty about facts and explanations concerning any matter being examined. When addressing controversial issues, teachers can pose questions that challenge students to examine a broad range of relevant evidence and empirical justifications, seeking to make valid judgments about the merits of competing claims. Employing a potentially helpful acronym, it might be said that in this examination process, students make a **PACT** with fair-minded, truth-seeking inquiry. That is, students actively aspire to identify the Pros (or factual validity) of various claims, examine any factual Ambiguities associated with particular claims, and identify the Cons of particular claims with reference to persuasive counterarguments. This commitment to practice these **PAC** considerations is an exemplary Truth-seeking treatment of the relevant factual evidence. **PACT** practices are designed to minimize the very human but often corrupting influences of impulsive, unreflective, bias-driven, and/ or tribal predeterminations that undermine the ideals of thoughtful, fair-minded engagements.

Definitional issues *arise when people* ascribe different meanings to similar terms. This type of interpretive diversity is quite ubiquitous. *Democracy, patriotism, equality, freedom, fairness, courage,* etcetera can be interpreted in multiple ways. The list of terms, ideas, and concepts that are potentially contested is virtually interminable. Causes for such contestation are many because words have multiple connotations, ranging from favorable to unfavorable, and are variable based on individuals' diverse experiences and particular intentions. Whether deliberate or unintentional, definitional problems can be significant in fomenting communicative misunderstanding and/or deception. In addressing definitional issues, teachers can seek to elicit the explicit interpretative meanings that individuals attribute to certain terms and to probe for possible conflicting perspectives and common ground. It may be necessary for teachers to stipulate a particular interpretation as a starting point for fair-minded engagements.

Value issues *perpetually arise as individuals and communities attempt to pursue diverse conceptions of the good life. In the abstract, many values can be seen as unequivocally desirable, such as freedom, security, peace, and fellowship. However, tensions arise when, in concrete cases, these otherwise desirable values conflict since prioritizing one value may entail subordinating and perhaps denying the validity of competing values. Teachers can seek to engage students in identifying the pertinent values in tension and to facilitate students'* consideration of why one set of values should or shouldn't take moral priority over others. Moreover, as catalysts for stimulating curiosity and nurturing nuance over predetermined dogmatism, teachers can honor the presence of ambivalence and ambiguity as arguably inherent dynamics tethered to complex matters of democratic living. Being sensitive to complexity and supportive of the dignity toward others can encourage a win-win mentality and promote a compelling constellation of values, including empathy, deep listening, recognition of common-ground perspectives, respect for deeply felt differences, judicious decision-making, and fair-minded compromise. In energizing these "better angels of our nature," teachers can adeptly seek to hold at bay corrosive and countervailing forces such as dogmatism, arrogance, power-domination and demonization of the Other.

The pedagogical artistry of cultivating these factual, definitional and value engagements is guided by a *search for unity in diversity*, which is the title of a book examining John Dewey's conception of democratic dialectics. The author of this text, James Good (2006), summarizes Dewey's dialectical perspective as follows:

> Dewey believed that when properly reconstructed, experience yields truth . . . in the sense of satisfaction or unification of the self in its never-ending efforts to cope with and, ideally, find harmony within its natural and social environment. . . . Self-development . . . is a striving toward one's potential, but it also includes *positive freedom*, understood as liberation through commitment to one's social responsibilities, and recognition of our worth by our peers.
>
> (246)

Abraham Lincoln's "Gettysburg Address" is a powerful illustration of practicing this positive freedom. Instead of engaging in a long-winded political speech condemning the Confederate states' violent secession, President Lincoln respectfully and prayerfully celebrates the soldiers who sacrificed their lives for their nation's democratic aspirations and then ends his funeral oration with a poetic, spiritual affirmation of Americans' capacities to pursue an inspired, inclusive unity:

> Four score and seven years ago, our fathers brought forth on this continent, a new nation, conceived in Liberty, and dedicated to the proposition that all men are created equal. Now we are engaged in a great civil war, testing whether that nation so conceived and so dedicated, can long endure. . . . We cannot dedicate—we cannot consecrate—we cannot hallow—this ground. The brave men, living and dead, who struggled here, have consecrated it, far above our poor power to add or detract. The world will little note, nor long remember what we say here, but it can never forget what they did here. It is for us the living, rather, to be dedicated here to the unfinished work which they who fought here have thus far so nobly advanced.

Lincoln's concluding sentence can be translated into a curriculum and teaching question that lies at the heart of the HI-STAR process: *Can we educators continue the "unfinished work" of advancing the Declaration of Independence's proposition that all men and women are created equal?* In John Dewey's language, can we facilitate educational experiences with the positive freedom of practicing unity within diversity? Though human differences are an ever-present reality of earthly living, can we build students' capacities to positively address this diversity through power-with engagements?

America's founding fathers understood that this positive freedom can easily get lost in the fog of religious dogmatism. They welcomed and respected religious inspiration but recognized that its dialectical cousin—a religious dogmatism that invites unbending theocratic imposition—is a looming presence in American life. Consequently, they constitutionally established the separation of church and state. Dewey explores the pedagogical implications of this constitutional decision in an essay titled *A Common Faith*. After making a distinction between unreflective religious dogma and thoughtful spiritual inspiration, Dewey argues that educators should consider how they can foster the heritage of inclusive religious values:

> [We educators have] the responsibility of conserving, transmitting, rectifying and expanding the heritage of values we have received that those who come after us may receive it more solid and secure, more widely accessible and more generously shared than we have received it. Here are all the elements for a religious faith that shall not be confined to sect, class, or race. Such a faith has always been implicitly the common faith of mankind. It remains to make it explicit and militant.
>
> (1934, 87)

Stanley (2024) concludes his astute critical analysis of fascism, which he defines as "one specific kind of authoritarian ideology" (p. xii), with a contemporary, compelling interpretation of the democratic common faith that Dewey celebrates. In the concluding chapter of his book, Stanley discusses how teachers can positively respond to the United States' drift toward fascism by pedagogically advancing "civic friendship . . . which signifies the underlying equality of regard which all persons are supposed to have for each other as citizens despite their diverse positions in the social division of labor" (175). He points out that "civic compassion" is a key feature of this teaching goal and presents a sociological insight into this key affective feature of educational ethic:

> Mutual estrangement and stereotypical fantasy exist between the extremes of our class structure, between several ethnic and racial groups

and between considerable numbers of males and females. This presents a major challenge for civic education, but it is not one of inducing some unrealistic and sentimental attitude of "unity." The challenge is the more difficult one of bringing people to the point of understanding the objective historical and existing conditions of groups with whom they have no personal life experience. Compassion presupposes the ability to "take the role of the other" in some particular and informed way.

(Stanley 1983, 872–73)

Stanley then presents his own succinct summary of civic compassion as the capacity "to engage respectfully, to imaginatively stand in the places of others, to inhabit worlds that initially seem strange and even threatening, to acknowledge one's inability to be as wise, as generous, or as open as pluralistic democracy requires" (176). This moral understanding provided the ethical guidance for Tom Kelly's and my lengthy deliberations on the purpose of practicing a democratic, dialectical mindfulness in education. It was an essential feature of the common faith that Tom and I share as we worked together on this section of chapter 6.

Envisioning a Pedagogical Application

I want to conclude my personal story with a description on how I would incorporate these six curriculum study themes into my teaching if I were not retired. As I have noted throughout this chapter, my personal narrative is built around my experiences with seven collaborative texts. I was the lead author in all these publication projects. Now that I am retired, I wanted to remove myself from such a leadership role, so Dan and Jen have taken the lead on this book. Though I wanted to stay in the background, they felt that I should compose this chapter to provide a historical, curriculum study context for the HI-STAR process we are advancing. It was my pleasure to accept their collegial invitation and to be able to celebrate an amazing generation of democratic educators that inspired my work. Though my academic studies are coming to a conclusion, Dan's and Jen's scholarly careers are just getting underway. The torch is passing to them, as it should. Democratic education in the United States and around the world is a multi-generational promise and challenge; and the way that Dan, Jen, and I have worked together on this book is a testament to this historical fact.

Speaking of passing the torch, I was part of the "Liberty Torch" relay team that ran non-stop through all 48 contiguous states over 47 summer days, celebrating the United States' 1976 Bicentennial Anniversary. We were thirty-three individual runners passing an actual torch to one another during five- to ten-mile runs. It was a joy sharing this Bicentennial celebration with my team members and, more significantly, with so many different Americans in more than one hundred small-town and large-city events. It's powerful democratic experience that I'll never forget. Here are excerpts from a "Letter of Commendation" that President Gerald R. Ford sent to the torch team before we began our relay run:

> We now mark the beginning of our Third Century as an Independent Nation as well as the 200th Anniversary of the American Revolution. For two centuries our nation has grown, changed and flourished. A diverse people, drawn from all corners of the earth, have joined together to fulfill the *promise of democracy*. . . . The Bicentennial offers each of us the opportunity to join with our fellow citizens in honoring the past and preparing for the future in communities across the Nation. . . . As we lay the cornerstone of America's Third Century, the very special part in this great national undertaking being performed by the Members of the Liberty Torch Bicentennial Group is most commendable.

What I want to highlight in these excerpts from President Ford's letter is his admiration for the "diverse" Americans who participated in advancing "the promise of democracy" between 1776 and 1976. At this current, tension-filled point in United States history, this is a quite relevant recognition by a GOP president, whose political party has its origins in Abraham Lincoln's presidency. Without President Lincoln's passionate, astute, and wise presidential leadership the United States' promise of democracy might have been a casualty of our country's civil war over human slavery. This possible historical outcome has present-day resonance since the current GOP has, arguably, become the "party of Trump" with its strong authoritarian agenda.

If I were not retired and still teaching experienced educators in my *Fundamentals of Curriculum* and *Curriculum Leadership* graduate courses at Kent State University, I would be quite excited about using our new book as a practical guide on how to create a Holistic, Imaginative (**HI**) curriculum platform supporting democratic, integrated Study, Teaching, Assessing, and Reflecting (**STAR**) activities. I would begin both graduate courses by reminding my students that the US Constitution, which is the longest continuous democratic constitution in human history, has the four foundational guardrails that I have already introduced in this chapter.

I would then present four ethical principles that are concise "expressive outcomes" (Eisner, 1994a) of my many years of curriculum studies, and I would undertake this introduction in a particular historical way. I would first ask my students to carefully read the first two chapters of Dewey's (1909/1933) *How We Think: A Restatement of the Relation of Reflective Thinking to the Educative Process*. We would discuss his argument that productive educational reflections by teachers and their students are guided by open-minded, whole-hearted, and responsible inquiries. Dewey describes these personal commitments as "attitudes that are favorable to the use of the best methods of inquiry" (29–30). He explains:

> Because of the importance of attitudes, ability to train thought is not achieved merely by knowledge of the best forms of thought. Possession of this information is no guarantee for ability to think well. Moreover, there are no set exercises in correct thinking whose repeated performance will cause one to be a good thinker. The information and the exercises are both of value. But no individual realizes their value except as he is personally animated by certain dominant attitudes in his own character.
>
> (29)

I would tell my students that I prefer the concept of "principles" over "attitudes" because I think it better captures the personal integrity—the **ethical character**—that democratic educators must cultivate. I want teachers and their supportive administrators to think of themselves as principled professionals, not semiprofessional workers compliantly submitting to authoritarian systems. However, I would invite my graduate students to work with whatever ethical perspectives they feel best informs their beliefs and images of democratic teaching.

I would explain that my platform beliefs and images are the product of fifty-six years of curriculum study and can be summarized as an interrelated set of professional ethics:

- *Practicing and teaching reflective inquiries*, as theorized, explained, and illustrated by John Dewey and Frank Ryan;
- *Practicing and teaching caring affirmations*, as theorized, explained, and illustrated by Nel Noddings;
- *Practicing and teaching expressive engagements*, as theorized, explained, and illustrated by Elliot Eisner;
- *Practicing and teaching fair-minded judgments*, as theorized, explained, and illustrated by Fred Newmann and Jason Stanley.

I would note that this ethical framework, which is an artifact of my many years of disciplined curriculum study, is based on the recognition that democratic teachers need to inquire into and embody the values they are overtly and tacitly advancing through their instruction. I believe that democratic teaching and learning are intimately connected. Teachers must model the values they are promoting; and in this way, their instruction has an authentic moral grounding. I would clarify this discussion by quoting Ryan (2011) on Dewey's understanding of how genuine values are realized through a life of authentic inquiry:

We have basic biological desires . . . which Dewey calls "impulses." But only a child . . . would mistake these for values. "I want it! I want it!" expresses an impulse or preference—something desir*ed*, but not necessarily *desirable*; something valu*ed*, though by no means *valuable*. . . . Recognizing the difference between what we happen to value at the beginning of inquiry and what proves to be valuable at its end, Dewey distinguishes a *value candidate* from a genuine *value* or good.

(64–65)

I would then introduce a set of study (S) activities that are my course-specific applications of the general practical, personal, critical, dialectical, communicative, and ecological inquiries introduced in chapter 5. I would explain that this multidimensional disciplined study is an educational application of the historic tradition of Socratic inquiry into human goodness (Henderson and Kesson 2004). It is designed to help them conceptualize and enact their "genuine values" as democratic educators in the face of dogmatic authoritarian pressures. In *Open Socrates: The Case for a Philosophic Life*, Agnes Callard (2025) provides a contemporary explanation and illustration of open-minded Socratic inquiry. She writes:

Socrates discovered that between the acknowledgement of one's own ignorance and the ideally knowledgeable life lies substantive ethics of inquiry. The way to be good when you don't know how to be good is by learning. . . .The Socratic view is that real courage and moderation and piety and justice are manifested in speech, and, more specifically, in the back-and-forth of inquisitive refutation. Socrates is making the radical claim that, for ignorant people like us, human goodness is primarily expressed in how a person conducts herself in inquiry, and that conversation is where we find our true home. This amounts to the Socratization of the whole of life.

(16, 249)

As they proceed with this openly liberalized and multifaceted study, I would explain that this course does not include a practicum component, so we won't be engaged in applying their inquiry studies to specific teaching (T) practices. However, they may want to create an instructional unit plan to help them better understand and envision their inquiries. If they voluntarily choose to take this step, they will have the opportunity to make a virtual presentation of their unit planning to their course colleagues. I know from my many years of graduate teaching that these inquiry activities may feel somewhat complicated and challenging at the beginning of the semester. Therefore, I will ask my graduate students to be patient with any cognitive dissonance they might be experiencing. I would let them know that I am deliberatively working with Andrea English's (2013) definition of *transformative learning*:

When teachers interrupt learners' experiences and allow them to feel the excitement of inquiry into the interruption, learners begin to trust the process of learning. The excitement experienced by learners is part of their becoming aware that, as individuals, their perspectives can change, they can come to see things differently, and that new encounters with otherness can lead them to call things into question. . . . When we view learning as transformative, then we can begin to see that we can actively seek out the new and unfamiliar—the otherness within oneself and within society—and embrace it as a possibility for transforming individual and social experiences.

(151–52)

I would assure my students that, as they proceed with the transformative learning in the course, the democratically principled approach to education that I am advancing will become clearer and clearer. I will tell them that it is my hope that, by the end of the semester, they will become quite comfortable with the idea of practicing their instructional responsibilities—teaching mathematics, teaching literature, teaching history, etc.—in their own democratically holistic, imaginative, and inquiring ways. They will come to appreciate how the *Anti-Authoritarian Curriculum Practice* text is designed to nurture and support their capacities to practice a democratic teaching artistry. I would also honestly acknowledge that this way of educating may need to be thoughtfully and gradually incorporated into classroom cultures—particularly given our country's heritage of standardized teaching policies, currently compounded by our society's growing moral nihilism (Hunter 2024). As they work on applying the HI-STAR process in their work settings, they may need to be creative in identifying where they have "wiggle room" to pursue this pedagogical artistry.

Because I'm teaching experienced teachers and educational administrators in these two graduate courses, my assessment and reflection (A&R) applications would be designed for mature adults. If I were teaching younger K–12 and college undergraduate students, the A&R activities I will briefly describe here would need to be adjusted in developmentally appropriate, concrete-operational ways. For my assessment (A) applications, I would begin by explaining to my graduate students that, as we proceed, it's important that we collegially assess their growth in understanding the four ethical principles, as well as any additional ethical insights they may have. For this purpose, I would ask them to create small working groups of four to five class members to discuss the assessment questions in chapter 5. Our assessment activities would end at this point; however, I would explain that if this graduate course included a practicum, we would take the next application step of teaching an actual 3S understanding unit and then collegially assessing its pedagogical artistry. To illustrate this scenario,

I would describe how I practiced such a collegial assessment with the California elementary school teacher in my dissertation research, which I briefly described earlier in this chapter.

After introducing a handout summarizing Eisner's (2017) four "dimensions" of educational criticism: description, interpretation, evaluation, and thematics, I would describe how I practiced this four-dimensional assessment over a two-year period that culminated with a descriptive essay, titled "An Educational Criticism of Miss R's Second Grade Classroom."

For my reflection (**R**) applications, I would first introduce them to the preface in Sean Wilentz's 2005 award-winning text, *The Rise of American Democracy: Jefferson to Lincoln*, which includes this insightful statement:

> Democracy is never a gift bestowed by benevolent, farseeing rulers who seek to reinforce their own legitimacy. It must always be fought for, by political coalitions that cut across distinctions of wealth, power, and interest. It succeeds and survives only when it is rooted in the lives and expectations of its citizens and is continually reinvigorated in each generation. Democratic successes are never irreversible.
>
> (xix)

I would then plan one or more reflective activities guided by the following five questions: Before taking this graduate course, have I ever experienced "democracy . . . as a way of *personal life* and one which provides a moral standard for *personal conduct*" (Dewey [1939] 1989, 101)? If so, how? If not, why do I think this is the case? Am I now optimistic about being able to build my capacities to teach a democratic, holistically integrated "subject, self, and social (3S) understanding" (Henderson 2001; Henderson and Gornik, 2007) that is grounded in continuous, interactive "educative experiences" (Dewey [1938] 1998)? If not, why do I feel that I can't undertake this professional development beyond this course introduction?

Recognizing that these five questions point to the personal developmental challenges embedded in this book's HI-STAR process, Tom Kelly and I decided to create a dialectical framework that introduces and conceptualizes the four ethical principles as four **ethical growth principles**. Our goal in taking this step is to provide additional guidance on how to address the above reflective questions through a long-term, continuing engagement in the HI-STAR process. I would ask my graduate students to read the following framework on how the four ethical principles—an expressive outcome of my disciplined curriculum studies—can be interpreted as ethical growth principles. I would give the students a week to study and take notes on this framework; we would then spend the next class session discussing their reflections.

Important distinctions about the above four ethical principles call for greater elaboration. In terming these concepts ethical growth principles, we are alluding to the notions that, regarding growth: (a) there is a continuum along which individuals display, to greater and lesser degrees, the characteristics associated with the particular principle; (b) there continually exist opportunities for individuals to enhance and, conversely, to diminish their commitment and capacities to possess and display the relevant characteristics; and (c) the characteristics of the higher end of the continuum are deemed significantly desirable while the lower end characteristics are immature or underdeveloped manifestations of the desirable principle. They are semi-ethical qualities needing to be outgrown and overcome. Let's examine the upper and lower ends of each principle's growth continua with the goal of illuminating important dimensions of each.

Advancing Reflective Inquiries: From the Cursory to the Robust

Though no one typology may satisfy all thoughtful analysts regarding any of the four proposed ethical growth principles, we offer the following conceptualization as a reasonable starting point for thinking about central dimensions and contrasting poles of reflective inquiry. The quality of one's inquiry may vary in terms of its depth or rigor (from superficial to sophisticated), its breadth (from selective to comprehensive), its deliberateness (from impulsive and scattered to thoughtful and systematic), its constructive criticality (from rubber-stamping to judicious skepticism), its overall creative resourcefulness (from passive to imaginative exploration of alternatives), according to whether one is considering the meaning or truthfulness of particular ideas or evaluating the evidence, possible conflicts of interest, and preexisting preferences or biases of specific claims.

Nurturing Caring Affirmations: From the Dismissive to the Dignifying

Potentially caring relationships may vary along a number of important dimensions: their trustworthiness (from being seen as deceitful, manipulative and/or unreliable to being seen as honest, respectful and dependable), their patterns of confirmation (from a tendency to impute bad-faith intentions to a presumption of good faith motivation), their constructive interpersonal sensitivity (from inattentiveness and/or self-absorption to empathetic perceptiveness), their conflict resolution dynamic (from strict avoidance, insincere sugar-coating, demonizing, and/or passive-aggressiveness to constructive candor and synergistic problem-solving), and their overall mutually supportive interaction (from selfishness and stinginess to generous responsiveness to a partner's needs).

Designing Expressive Engagements: From Standardization to Student Voice and Choice

Given the potential inspirational power of walking one's own talk and the significant instructive power of directly experiencing the alleged benefits and compelling challenges of preeminent curricular aims (e.g., the desirability and demands of democracy), educators providing students meaningful, appropriately guided opportunities to exercise voice and choice in the educational process would seem to be a consummate characteristic of education in and for a democracy.

The opportunities for such voice and choice are ubiquitous and prodigious. A suggestive, if partial and overlapping list of opportunities would include:

1. types of learning activities (teacher- or student-led lectures and discussions, group work, audio-visual presentations, individual work);

2. forms of representing understanding of studied material (written prose/poetry, oral speech/song, artistic/computer graphics, dramatic skit);

3. achievement incentives and celebrations;

4. deadlines and extension policies;

5. class norms;

6. consequences for norm violations;

7. classroom service committees and leadership positions;

8. valid extra credit experiences;

9. overall categories for grade determination and their relative weighting.

One can imagine a range of quality implementation associated with these opportunities in terms of their organization (from haphazard to well-managed), clarity (from confusing to well-articulated), and balance of potential competing values (from unconstrained student control to unresponsive teacher control). Organized, clear, and judiciously balanced implementation is thoughtfully justified, perceptively assessed, sensitively refined, and responsive to high-performance standards by respectful teachers' responsiveness and support.

Fostering Fair-Minded Judgments: From Narrow and Narcissistic Considerations to Compassionate and Fair Decision-Making

A close and perhaps not fully distinguishable kin to reflective inquiry, this principle complements the reflective inquiry focus on truth, factual accuracy, evidential support, and clear definition of terms with an insistent commitment to fairness and justice. Compatible with both Fred Newmann's scholarship on addressing controversial public issues (1970) and the ethical decision-making framework provided by the Markkula Center for Applied Ethics (2021), this growth principle emphasizes a requisite inclusiveness and impartiality in arriving at ethically valid conclusions, filtering such deliberations through the several historical lenses that have come to characterize the field of ethical decision-making. These perspectives include the rights lens, the justice lens, the utilitarian lens, the common good lens, the virtue lens, and the care ethics lens.

In its clear-eyed commitment to inclusive impartiality, at least two overlapping paths of growth are characteristic of this principle. The first is more related to the process of inquiry, in which growth proceeds from bias-confirming, self-centered, self-deceptive, possibly self-aggrandizing conclusion-drawing toward rigorous, explicitly fair-minded consideration of competing perspectives. The second path is more related to the achievement of panoramic and profound inquiry, where growth proceeds from ignorance or some distortion (unintentional or otherwise) of the invariably multiple perspectives deserving due consideration around a controversial decision toward a nuanced, empathetic portrayal/representation of each of the diverse perspectives in play. In this second scenario, at least ideally, an exemplary representative of each of the pertinent perspectives, in giving truthful feedback to the person seeking to accurately portray the representative's point of view, would be in the position to say something like: "I must say that you appear to understand my perspective exceptionally well."

I want to conclude my curriculum study story with a personal plea to all current and future generations of educators who work in societies with democratic constitutions. No matter what professional challenges we educators may face, please keep in mind that we need to embrace and persistently cultivate our democratic character and pedagogical artistry. After all, what's the alternative? It's a historical fact that democracy is a very difficult and messy way of governing; but it is arguably still better than all other political alternatives. As the "founding fathers" of the American constitution noted, we humans are not perfect. However, despite their realistic concerns, they were hopeful that the new United States' promise of democracy with its holistic, imaginative vision of "life, liberty, and the pursuit of happiness" for all Americans would blossom. Shouldn't this inclusive visionary hopefulness be the moral compass for our curriculum and teaching work? The following excerpt from a letter that Thomas Jefferson (1786) sent to a colleague on the vital importance of public education in the new American nation historically and emphatically informs this ethical question:

> No other sure foundation can be devised for the preservation of freedom, and happiness. . . . Preach, my dear Sir, a crusade against ignorance; establish and improve the law for educating the common people. Let our countrymen know that the people alone can protect us against [authoritarian leaders] . . . and that the tax which will be paid for this purpose is not more than the thousandth part of what will be paid to kings, priests and nobles who will rise up among us if we leave the people in ignorance.
>
> (para. 3)

7

Building on and Extending a Curriculum Legacy

Curriculum . . . [is] the site on which the generations struggle to define themselves and the world.

(PINAR ET AL. 1995, 847–48)

Education, curriculum, teaching, and learning are intergenerational phenomena and part of our individual and collective dynamic dance toward more wisdom as human beings, the evolution in our thoughts, actions, and hearts. As educators we live, create meaning, and make decisions as part of an ever-evolving world, and this process is rife with tension, disappointment, and uncertainty but also with joy, fulfillment, and hope. We stand at an intersection of what is known and what is unknown and even what is unknowable. We navigate the revibrating effects of what happened before us within the contexts, circumstances, situations, and relationships of our own times. We build upon previous generations' insights while also challenging and reimagining the possibilities for educational futures. While doing this, we also walk alongside students, supporting their growth with subject matter understanding while doing what we can to help them along their own unique paths in the world. Consider your own educational experiences and the intergenerational web that has shaped not only you as an educator and learner, but the broader educational landscape in which you participate. Who are the educators and mentors that shape your understanding of what education is and what it might become? How do they echo in your thoughts and actions in the present? What values have you come to understand or question through them about what education is?

The opening quote to this chapter touches upon the intergenerational quality of education and being an educator, and it comes from a curriculum studies tome titled, *Understanding Curriculum* that was authored by

William Pinar, William Reynolds, Patrick Slattery, and Peter Taubman some thirty years ago in 1995. Their book was a significant contribution to the field of curriculum studies and supported generations of thinkers toward complicating conversations about curriculum. Reconceptualization, as touched upon in prior chapters of this book, sought to challenge and transform traditional notions of curriculum. Curriculum was repositioned as more than a static thing, such as a textbook, handout, quiz, or lesson plan. Curriculum was more than prescriptions of what and how to teach. Curriculum was more than preparing students for standardized tests and teachers delivering subject matter content linearly through narrowly defined objectives or mandates given from top-down systems like government departments and accreditation bodies. Curriculum was more than efficiency and measurements for effectiveness that treat education as a system and the people in it (teachers and students) in need of being controlled. Curriculum became much broader. It was positioned as a verb, as lived experience, and as multidimensional, meaning psychological, cultural, moral, historical, political, temporal, aesthetic, and more all at once. Reconceptualization emphasized the importance and interconnectedness of these factors, advocating for educators to reflect the richness of lived experience and the pursuits of social critique and personal inner growth.

This book that you are reading with its HI-STAR process and starter kit of six forms of curriculum inquiry (i.e., practical, personal, critical, communicative, dialectical, and ecological) has roots in the momentum from reconceptualization while also drawing heavily on thinkers like Decker Walker and Joseph Schwab who are often not considered reconceptualists. The HI-STAR process embraces a holistic and imaginative understanding of curriculum and strives to support educators' personal democratic growth alongside social critique. While reconceptualization aimed to transcend more traditional views of curriculum, this book does the opposite in recognizing the ongoing need to engage with traditional, technical viewpoints. After all, they often reflect the day-to-day demands, expectations, and realities many educators face. This feels particularly pressing now as educational practices, policies, and governance are increasingly leaning toward authoritarian tendencies that favor control, obedience, punishment, hegemony, surveillance, and compliance. Such tendencies come at the expense of nurturing more democratic ethics, overshadowing values like those of humility, compassion, criticality, difference, creative expression, curiosity, and wonder.

Conceptualizing the connections between democratic ethics and education has been a central pillar in Jim's educational journey and scholarly thought on the nature of curriculum. His narrative in chapter 6 beautifully traces his beginning thinking about this educational problem during his time at liberal arts institutions and later in his career supporting educators' pedagogical artistry at Kent State University (KSU). Jim has been a tremendous teacher and mentor for us, Jen and Dan (who are the authors of this chapter). We would likely not be engaged in curriculum studies if it were not for his presence in our educational journeys. We were first introduced to the field of curriculum studies in the early 2000s while taking graduate courses Jim taught at KSU, specifically *Fundamentals of Curriculum* as well as *Theory and Research in Curriculum*. Even though we each went through teacher preparation programs—Dan in early childhood and Jen in art education— neither of us had heard of curriculum studies prior to those courses we took with Jim. More than once, we have with curiosity and frustration remarked to each other and to Jim, "Why did I not know about curriculum studies before doing a PhD?" Through curriculum studies and our collaboration with Jim during our doctoral studies and beyond, we uncovered a wealth of intellectually stimulating ideas and questions that profoundly deepened and broadened our understanding of curriculum. As part of the current generation of curriculum thinkers, we can confidently say that both Jim's scholarship on democratic education, curriculum leadership, and pedagogical artistry have had a lasting influence on our thinking.

Worth highlighting are two books we collaborated on that predate this project. In the edited volume *Reconceptualizing Curriculum Development* (Henderson et al. 2015), we wrote chapters focused on reflective inquiry in curriculum and its development. Dan's chapter illuminated how educators could engage with democratic reflection in their own teaching, in classrooms and with students. Jen's chapter explored how educators could reflectively cultivate their own inner awareness for embodying democratic education. Several years later, in 2018, we partnered with Jim again and explored democratic values in education and leadership through tackling the area of educational problem-solving. In that book, titled *Democratic Curriculum Leadership*, we argued for a shift away from problem-solving that wants quick fixes and is mechanical and linear toward a more humanizing, recursive, and collaborative problem-solving. We curated study and practice guidance to support educators with such problem-solving. These two book projects led us into deeper understandings about democratic ethics and the ways in which curriculum is reflective, dialogical, and moral as well as personal, social, and political.

What we notice today is that educators and education are facing very trying times and growing challenges with political polarization, misinformation, societal inequalities, mental and physical well-being crises, and the environmental crisis. We witness authoritarian tendencies and practices in educational governance rapidly blooming around us. We also hear about these from the educators we work with every day, and we, too, experience the various crises and reverberating affects and effects of authoritarian practices in our own lives. We are concerned about the future for democratic ethics in the United States and abroad. The rise of authoritarianism is part of the reason why this book does not prescribe a specific model of democratic education or dictate which democratic ethics educators should believe in—an approach that would be undemocratic. Instead, it focuses on supporting educators with thoughtful curriculum engagement. Through curriculum engagement, educators can create spaces for themselves and with others where their democratic understandings can thrive, and their critical, reflective, creative thinking can help them navigate increasing authoritarian pressures as best as they can from their specific contexts.

Portals and Reflections: Democracy Ethics in Curriculum and Teaching

In the remainder of this chapter, we reflect on the enduring value and relevance of the curriculum studies legacy we encountered through thinking and working alongside Jim, even as we grapple with it in the present. We highlight aspects of his mentorship and teachings that have served as democratic portals including: an eclectic-holistic spirit, reflective awareness, and hope. The three portals are not meant to imply a specific destination as if they could magically teleport you to the answers on how to embody democracy. They are more like doorways that have opened to vast, complicated spaces along our ongoing learning and growth with embodying democratic ethics. They are also ways in which Jim's embodiment of a democratic ethic has been demonstrated. While our experiences with these portals have shaped our journeys, we simply offer them to you as invitations to consider. As you engage with challenges and joys of democratic ethics for yourself, consider what doorways might have been opened for you, leading to new opportunities for reflection, growth, and action in your practice.

Portal One: A Holistic-Eclectic Spirit

An enduring aspect we find compelling and consistently admire about the curriculum legacy we've learned through our work with Jim is his commitment to embracing eclecticism and holism when theorizing and teaching about curriculum. A holistic-eclectic spirit can be described as a practice of drawing from diverse ideas, perspectives, and approaches to integrate them into a unified whole that is always evolving and coming into being. This portal opens to possibilities of integrating pieces into a greater whole while resisting narrow or dogmatic thinking. Jim's influence has always encouraged us to seek unity through diversity, to see the connections between seemingly disparate ideas, and to understand that no single approach or framework can capture the full complexity of democratic education.

In the curriculum studies literature, particularly since the reconceptualization of the field, many scholars have debated the contributions of past figures like Ralph Tyler for example whose work has been critiqued, perhaps even villainized, for being too technical and rational. Tyler, a thinker that shaped twentieth-century educational thought, promoted a framework for problem-solving and curriculum development that emphasized: What are the educational goals, what experiences will achieve them, how should these experiences be organized, and how can we assess their success? (Tyler 1949). Jim consistently pushed against the trend of "throwing the baby out with the bathwater." He recognizes the importance in Tyler's ideas, while simultaneously challenging the rigid, rationalistic methods that often underpinned them. In witnessing Jim do this we recognize a humanizing quality of a holistic-eclectic spirit. In *Democratic Curriculum Leadership* (2018), Tyler's framework was reimagined, stripping away the technical rationality that has dominated its use in modern educational systems. Jim's work has consistently pushed us toward seeing and thinking about correlatives and relationships between (both/and) things rather than getting stuck in dualism (either/or).

A holistic-eclectic spirit also shines in how Jim has consistently drawn upon a wide array of curriculum thinkers, weaving them together into a tapestry for democratic education, including but not limited to Nel Noddings, Maxine Greene, James Macdonald, and Elliot Eisner. But Jim's eclectic approach extends beyond the curriculum theorists. In chapter 6, Jim reflects on his engagements with broader intellectual traditions. John Dewey's focus on integrating logic and moral character is central to Jim's thinking, as is Herbart's notion of transformative, dialectical learning. Jim also highlights more contemporary thinkers like Luc Ferry, who promotes a vision of democratic education rooted in humanism, and Doris Kearns Goodwin, whose historical narratives of democratic leadership, particularly her work on Abraham Lincoln, resonate with Jim's understanding of education as an ethical practice. Engagement with diverse thinkers (dead and alive) is a way into the portal of an eclectic, holistic spirit. Through deliberation and dialogue among multiple perspectives, understandings of democratic education and its ethical dimensions can be deepened.

In a time when education is increasingly governed by rigid frameworks, efficiency metrics, and authoritarian tendencies, a holistic-eclectic spirit offers a powerful counterpoint. It does not deny such realities in education, while at the same time challenging them through reaffirming the importance of creativity, criticality, and humanity in education. In previous chapters, we explored how curriculum is more than a set of prescribed content or outcomes; it is a lived, multidimensional experience—an evolving dance between the personal and the social, between individual growth and collective responsibility. An eclectic-holistic spirit aligns with these values, embracing the tension and complexity of education rather than reducing it to narrow metrics. As we discussed in chapters 1 through 5, democratic education asks us to be open to diverse perspectives and attuned to the evolving needs of our students and society. In this way, eclecticism and holism resist authoritarian tendencies that prioritize control and uniformity, offering instead an invitation to engage with the world's richness, uncertainty, and possibility.

As we consider this portal, we see it as a space where we are invited to practice an ever-deepening inquiry into what it means to educate democratically. This portal represents not only a collection of diverse ideas but a commitment to nurturing openness, adaptability that welcomes the complexities of curriculum theory and practice. We view a holistic-eclectic spirit as more than just a theoretical framework; it is a lived, intentional approach that we will continually refine and expand over the course of our careers as educators. In our teaching, we hope to guide our students to engage with their own holistic-eclectic spirits actively, encouraging them to explore the intersections between theory and practice, to question assumptions of institutions, others, and themselves, and to find their own ways to integrate diverse perspectives into their evolving visions of democratic education. As you reflect on this portal, we invite you to consider it as well and leave some questions here for you to consider in relationship to your own curriculum journey and anti-authoritarian practice.

- How might a holistic-eclectic spirit already be part of your own educational practice? Are there ways you might be limiting this, consciously or unconsciously? Why do you think that is?

- What diverse influences can you draw upon to enrich your approach to teaching and learning? Can you think of a time when a more holistic, eclectic approach led to a breakthrough in your teaching and/or curriculum design?

- How might a spirit of eclecticism or holism help you resist the pressures of ideological rigidity and authoritarianism in your educational context?

- What tensions exist between the practical demands of your educational context and your desire for a more holistic approach? How might you navigate these tensions to move toward a more holistic practice?

- How might you take one step toward incorporating a more eclectic-holistic spirit in your teaching or curriculum?

Portal Two: Reflective Awareness

Another empowering aspect of Jim's work that we consistently admire is his dedication to fostering reflective awareness on curriculum and pedagogy in relationship to democracy. His work always emphasizes the importance of ongoing self and social examination. Much like a holistic-eclectic spirit, reflective awareness is a practice that invites educators to engage in continuous self-reflection and critical inquiry. This portal invites educators to engage in the ongoing process through examining their own practices, habits, beliefs, actions, and broader educational contexts. It involves thoughtful questioning, self-evaluation, and the exploration of how teaching methods, curriculum decisions, and interactions with students align with ethical and democratic principles. Reflective awareness encourages continuous learning and adaptation, fostering growth both for educators and their students. This reflection is also not just an intellectual process in the mind, but it can create changes in how we act and respond to circumstances and our relationships with ourselves and others. It is an inherently humanizing practice that invites educators to cultivate relationships rooted in care, respect, and compassion.

Jim's commitment to reflective inquiry has been central to his career, a point he delves into in detail in chapter 6 but also in other projects we have worked with him on (Henderson, et al. 2015; Henderson, Castner, and Schneider 2018). He draws deeply on the work of John Dewey, particularly Dewey's ideas on inquiry and reflection. Dewey emphasized that genuine reflective thinking emerges when seemingly easy solutions aren't available or when something "stings"—a disruption in the usual way of doing things. Dewey's circuit of inquiry—which involves recognizing a problematic situation, devising a hypothesis, and testing it—has greatly influenced Jim's work. Dewey also introduced a circuit of valuation, where ethical reflection is integral to the inquiry process (Ryan 2011). Building on these foundations, Jim advocates for educators to engage in ethical inquiry and deliberations. In this way, educators not only work to solve problems but also engage in ethical reflection on the degree to which their decisions foster and embody democratic ethics.

A core theme in much of Jim's work that we find important for navigating the current growing authoritarian tendencies is supporting reflective awareness that is humanizing in nature. Noddings's (2001) exploration of care and coercion in education is helpful here. She critiques how coercive educational practices, such as rigid curricula and standardized testing, are often justified in the name of "caring" for students' futures. However, she argues that genuine care must be relational, not imposed. In this light, reflective awareness becomes a way for educators to examine whether their practices are meeting the needs of their students or if they are imposing one-size-fits-all solutions that neglect students' individual experiences and humanity.

Reflective awareness infused with humanizing qualities encourages educators to engage with the human dimensions of teaching, recognizing that learning is not just about intellectual development but also emotional, social, and moral growth. Noddings's concept of relational care—where the carer must attentively listen to and respond to the needs of the cared-for—serves as a guide for reflection. Care, as Noddings describes, requires compassion and responsiveness to individual needs that are part of a relationship. Relational care, embedded in reflective practice, fosters an ethical dimension where educators move beyond technical efficiency, nurturing the well-being and dignity of themselves, students, and others. By incorporating caring into reflective practice, educators create spaces where all voices are valued; differences are embraced; and the emotional, social, and intellectual dimensions of existence are nurtured. Reflective awareness, then, becomes not only a critical tool but a form of ethical engagement that directly counters the dehumanizing forces present in authoritarianism.

Reflective awareness plays a vital role in education against authoritarianism because it empowers both educators and students to critically examine their own beliefs and practices as well as the structures around them. In chapters 1 through 5, we explore how democratic ethics require continuous reflection on issues such as power dynamics, agency, and the role of curriculum in fostering critical thinking. Reflection is encouraged as a counter to authoritarian tendencies, which often promote obedience, conformity, passivity, and control. Through reflective awareness, educators are encouraged to question top-down mandates, rigid standards, narrow definitions of success, and much more. Reflection, as highlighted throughout the HI-STAR process, aligns with democratic ethics by promoting dialogue, self-awareness, and ethical engagement. It encourages educators to view their practice as fluid, evolving, and responsive to the needs of their students and the complexities of society. By fostering reflective awareness, educators create spaces where students can also engage with these questions, empowering them to resist authoritarian influences and explore what living more democratically might look and feel like.

Within this portal, we see reflective awareness as an essential, ongoing practice for engaging with and embodying a democratic ethic. We strive to continuously cultivate our own awarenesses and to support the educators we work with to do the same. By fostering spaces where educators can explore and challenge educational beliefs, assumptions, and practices, we hope that reflective awareness might continue to enrich their personal and professional growth. In our teaching, we also encourage educators to see reflective awareness as both an individual and shared journey of ethical inquiry—one that invites them to engage more deeply with democratic ethics in ways meaningful to them. As you consider the portal of reflective awareness in your own practice, we invite you to think more about how ongoing self-examination, critical inquiry, and ethical reflection can help you navigate the complexities of democratic education.

- How might engaging in reflective awareness help you challenge authoritarian tendencies within your educational context?
  How might reflective awareness become a form of resistance in

environments that prioritize control over creativity or compliance over criticality?

- In what ways do you already incorporate self-reflection and critical inquiry into your practice? How might you expand these practices?

- How might your decisions be impacting not only intellectual outcomes but also the well-being and dignity of students? How might you foster spaces of care, dignity, and compassion for your students and for yourself?

- What roles do dialogue and deliberation play in your educational practice? How could fostering greater reflective awareness enable richer, more humanizing conversations that amplify diverse voices and perspectives?

- How can reflective awareness help you better understand and respond to the evolving needs of students and the complexities of society? What might you do (or try out) to make your practice a little more fluid and responsive rather than static or prescriptive?

Portal Three: Hope

Another deeply inspiring aspect of Jim's work that we admire is his unwavering belief in the power of hope as a driving force in education. We admire his commitment to hopefulness in democratic ethics, particularly as a practice that educators can embody in their daily work and relationships in the pursuit of a better future. Hope, much like reflective awareness and a holistic-eclectic spirit, is also a practice. Hope is a practice that invites educators to envision possibilities beyond the limitations of the present. A similar sentiment was echoed in Freire's (1994) reflections on hope as central to education. Hopefulness allows both educators and students to embrace a belief that change is possible, even in the face of overwhelming challenges and circumstances. Through hope we can resist authoritarian pressures and work toward a more democratic, just, and compassionate now amid our immediate relationships.

In educational discourse today, hope can often take a back seat to criticality. There is a lot of attention being given to identifying and deconstructing systems of oppression—systems that perpetuate capitalism, colonialism, classism, ablism, sexism, and racism—and rightfully so, given the way in which they exclude, atomize, objectify, and disempower. While critical examination is necessary, it can sometimes lead to a sense of nihilism or despair when solutions seem distant or impossible. The language and metaphors used in education can also draw on violence. For example, education is often portrayed as "under siege" or in "a war." Teachers and their work get described as being on the "front lines" and "in the trenches," and when they reach a certain point in their career they're called "veterans." Educational activism and activists use phrases like getting more "boots on the ground" and the emotional and psychological drain they experience gets called "battle fatigue." Much like the HI-STAR process, Jim's work does not succumb to nihilism or condone violence whether metaphorical or literal. He is walking a path of nonviolence (Wang 2024) as an educator, although he may not describe that in his narrative in chapter 6.

Nihilism can emerge when hope is overlooked in education. Nihilism implies a bleak outlook and the sense that nothing can change. It can also be part of our inner projections, our "shadow" (Jung 1970) that, for example, something is not happening "fast enough" or the "way it should be." Nihilism can be a significant psychological threat for both educators and students particularly in contexts where authoritarian practices are growing. Sustained nihilism can lead to feelings such as anxiety, depression, and disengagement, both from education and from broader social life. When educators or students adopt a nihilistic perspective, they lose deep connection with meaning, value, and purpose in their professional and personal lives. They may question the purpose of their efforts, asking, "What's the point of learning this if life has no ultimate meaning?" In this sense, nihilism can erode well-being, creating a cycle of apathy and disconnection. However, in the face of such despair, hope becomes not just a feeling but a vital practice—one that offers a way to resist the forces of nihilism and claim purpose and meaning. Where nihilism creates disconnection, hope fosters reconnection, both within us and with the world around us.

To clarify, this sense of hope is not bound by the need to control or dominate to get one's way. Václav Havel (1991, 181) famously wrote, "Hope is not the conviction that something will turn out well, but the certainty that something is worth doing no matter how it turns out." Havel's reflections on hope—developed during his struggle for human dignity and freedom in the oppressive context of the Communist regime in Czechoslovakia—resonate deeply with the challenges educators face today. For Havel, hope is not about expecting a positive outcome but about the moral responsibility to pursue meaningful action, even in the face of uncertainty. This kind of hopefulness seems to us to be an important part of democratic ethics and the transformational learning of the HI-STAR process. While the word *hopeium*—a blend of hope and opium—can be used to describe a naive or overly optimistic hope that clouds judgment, Jim has always seemed to approach hope as the opposite. His hopefulness is grounded in critical, reflective thinking and moral responsibility, rejecting false optimism and instead focusing on meaningful action, even when the outcomes are uncertain. Whereas hopeium leads to inaction, Jim's hopefulness empowers educators to take meaningful action, even in the smallest spaces available.

We have always recognized Jim's idea of "wiggle room" as central to the practice of democratic education. In the face of the growing momentum of authoritarianism, educators may feel as though the systems they operate within are increasingly rigid and oppressive. Jim emphasizes that while educators may not be able to change the entire system, there are always small spaces and times where they can act to foster democratic ethics. A helpful comparison is the maxim often widely associated with the twenty-sixth president of the United States, Teddy Roosevelt: "Do what you can, where you are, with what you have." This captures the essence of wiggle room. It's the idea that within even the most rigid systems, educators can create small sanctuaries of possibility, spaces where hopefulness and democratic ethics and action might thrive.

For example, a teacher might invite students to help shape class rules or choose between project options, giving them a voice in their learning. When a student challenges an idea from a required textbook, rather than shutting it down, a teacher might engage in discussion, modeling open inquiry. Instead of immediately resorting to punishment for misbehavior, a teacher might have conversations to better understand the root cause(s) and seek a restorative rather than punitive approach to classroom management. A teacher might invite students to draft potential test questions or collaboratively design a study guide, reinforcing the idea that assessment can be a shared process for learning rather than a "got you" moment on a test.

Even in what seem to be challenging situations and circumstances, we always have a choice. We might not be able to do certain things or everything we wish, but while we must remain aware of and attentive to the potential consequences of our action, we still have the power to interpret and respond to circumstances in meaningful ways (Frankl [1959] 2006). Though the momentum of authoritarian practices in education can feel overwhelming, hope allows us to reimagine what is possible and stay anchored in what is possible in the present moment (Hahn [1975] 1987; Tulku [1978] 1990). Hopefulness reminds us that within even the most constrained spaces, there are opportunities—however small—to act with integrity and to nurture curiosity and democratic ethics. Hopefulness is not passive; it is a deliberate stance, a commitment to seeing and cultivating possibility even in the face of rigidity. When the world outside feels chaotic or unchangeable, hope can become an act of resistance, a refusal to surrender the belief that change, however tiny, is still within reach.

We see hope as an important element of democratic education but also as a practice we explore alongside the educators we work with, supporting them to consider what might be doable within their here and now. Hope is not about wishful thinking or naive optimism but about critical, meaningful, purposeful action. In our teaching, we invite educators to find their own "wiggle room" within challenging systems, to identify small but meaningful spaces for action, and to question and seek out meanings, even in the face of uncertainty. Through this practice of hope, we aim to hold spaces where educators feel empowered to act as agents of change, fostering democratic ethics and purpose in their lives and the lives of their students. As you consider the portal of hope in your own practice and curriculum theorizing, we invite you to reflect on how cultivating hopefulness might inform your approach to curriculum, teaching, learning, and navigating the challenges of authoritarianism in education. Below are some questions to encourage you to think about how hopefulness can be an integral part of your democratic educational journey.

- How might you cultivate hopefulness in your teaching practice in ways that resist authoritarian pressures?
- What "wiggle room" exists within your current educational context, where you can create spaces for democratic ethics and meaningful action?
- How could you navigate the balance between critical examination of oppressive systems and fostering hope for change?
- In what ways can you help both yourself and your students resist the pull of nihilism and maintain a sense of meaning, purpose, and agency in the face of overwhelming challenges?

Conclusion: In Pursuit of a Loving Way

As we conclude this chapter and book, we hope that through the HI-STAR process, you have discovered meaningful pathways toward embodying democracy in your own teaching practice and that as you continue along your journey of curriculum understanding you continue to find inspiration. Democracy, at its core, is not simply a form of governance; it can also be understood as a way of knowing and being—a manifestation of what might be called "a loving way" of relating with others and the world. Throughout human existence, various philosophical, religious, and cultural traditions have emphasized "loving ways" as paths for ethical living together and well-being. Although the approaches vary across time and human civilizations, they are often grounded in respect for the dignity of all beings, kindness, and compassion.

Ahimsa is a fundamental principle of Indian philosophy that in its broadest sense is about respect for all living beings and the avoidance of harm. It's a practice that extends to every aspect of life, influencing the way people interact with one another and with nature. In various indigenous American traditions, loving ways manifest in the careful stewardship of the land and interpersonal relationships that honor equality, reciprocity, and the interconnectedness of all life. *Ubuntu* is a Southern African philosophy that can be summed up as "I am because we are." It emphasizes interconnectedness, community, and the inherent dignity of every person.

Agape is a Greek word for love that refers to unconditional, selfless love, often associated with the teachings of Jesus in Christianity through compassion and forgiveness. *Maitri* (loving-kindness) is from Buddhism and is the cultivation of an unconditional, universal love for all beings without any expectation of return or personal gain. In the context of education today, these historical and cultural examples remind us of the importance of fostering relationships based on mutual care, compassion, and shared senses of responsibility.

These traditions remind us that education, too, can embody a loving way—one that nurtures relationships built on care, mutual respect, and a shared sense of responsibility. Just as these philosophies honor the interconnectedness of life, democratic education can be a kind of loving way as well, where everyone is valued and where the cultivation of human dignity remains central. When democracy is rooted in care, criticality, compassion, and commitment to the well-being and dignity of all beings, it reflects a deep relational ethic that goes beyond governance and the mechanics of voting or policy-making—it embodies a respect for the voices, experiences, and humanity of each person even when there are differences and disagreements. As John Dewey (1916) reminds us, democracy is a mode of "associated living," an ongoing process that requires active participation, mutual understanding, and collective responsibility. This can be understood as a kind of love, where we engage with others not out of a desire for control or dominance, but out of a genuine commitment to individual and collective growth, flourishing, and empowerment.

In education, democracy as "a loving way" is reflected in democratic practices that foster dialogue, reflection, compassion, inclusion, and collaboration. Educators, for example, can create spaces where students' voices are heard and valued, where their unique potential is recognized, and where they are empowered to think critically and act with agency. Pedagogical practices like dialogue, active listening, authentic choice, contemplative practices, artmaking, or restorative justice in classrooms could become entrées to the loving way of democratic education. As Freire (1994) articulated, love is at the heart of any true educational endeavor—it is the driving force that nurtures both teacher and student in their shared journey toward freedom and self-actualization.

As educators, we should work to reject despair and embrace hope and love as active practices, continuously inviting ourselves, students, and others to envision a more just and humane future. A democratic education resists authoritarian practices and policies that rely on fear, silence, obedience, and control. Instead, it prioritizes humanization. It embraces the power of love over the love of power, recognizing all as inherently worthy of respect, expression, existence, compassion, and care. Democracy is not just a structure that societies craft into laws to live under or by; it is a way of being with our self and with others—a relational practice that seeks to uplift, nurture, and transform. It is, at its best, a loving way.

NOTES

Chapter 1

1 Basic curriculum problems include determining what is most worth knowing and experiencing in schools.

2 In the United States, curricula are influenced by both right-wing and left-wing educational reform activists. While progressive and left-wing activism is prominently situated in the academy, right-wing educational activism is supported by conservative think tanks and politicians.

3 Far too often, through so-called accountability-based policies, policymakers exercise authority to influence curriculum practices while sabotaging accountability for their decisions' effects. We define authoritarian practices as actions where accountability for how authority is exercised is sabotaged.

Chapter 4

1 These are our reinterpretations of the four traditions Null identified. We consider them four broad categories that helpfully scaffold a comprehensive consideration of theories of curriculum practice.

REFERENCES

Adler, M. 1982. *The Paideia Proposal: An Educational Manifesto*. Macmillan.

Arendt, H. 2006. *Eichmann in Jerusalem: A Report on the Banality of Evil*. Penguin Books.

Barton, K. C. 2024. "Knowledge Without Disciplines: A Critique of Social Realism's Disciplinary Fixation." *Journal of Curriculum Studies* 56 (3): 235–45 https://doi.org/10.1080/00220272.2024.2328058.

Berlin, I. 1953. *The Hedgehog and the Fox: An Essay on Tolstoy's View of History*. Weidenfeld & Nicolson.

Bernier, N. R., and J. E. Williams. 1973. *Beyond Beliefs: Ideological Foundations of American Education*. Prentice-Hall.

Biesta, G. 2024. "Taking Education Seriously: The Ongoing Challenge." *Educational Theory* 74 (3): 434–48.

Bloom. A. 1987. *The Closing of the American Mind*. Simon & Schuster.

Bobbitt, F. 1918. *The Curriculum*. Houghton Mifflin.

Brinton, C. 1965. *The Anatomy of Revolution*. Vintage.

Buber, M. 1965. *Between Man and Man*. Macmillan.

Callard, A. 2025. *Open Socrates: The Case for a Philosophical Life*. W. W. Norton & Company.

Castner, D. J. 2015. "Teaching for Holistic Understanding: Inspirational Events in Study and Practice." In *Reconceptualizing Curriculum Development: Inspiring and Informing Action*, edited by J. G. Henderson et al., 65–79. Routledge.

Castner, D. J. 2021. "Reconsidering Early Childhood Education Curriculum Leadership in Light of the Reconceptualization: Moving Beyond DAP Technologies." *International Critical Childhood Policy Studies Journal* 8 (2): 104–14.

Castner, D. J. 2022. "Fidelity in Teaching Young Children: Two Stories of Professional Integrity." *Journal of Research in Childhood Education* 36 (2): 239–54.

Castner, D. J., J. G. Henderson, and J. L. Schneider. 2020. "Curriculum Wisdom and Educational Leadership." In *Oxford Research Encyclopedia of Education*, edited by M. F. He and W. Schubert. Oxford University Press. doi:10.1093/acrefore/9780190264093.013.1049.

Castner, D. J., J. L. Schneider, and J. G. Henderson. 2017. "An Ethic of Democratic, Curriculum-Based Teacher Leadership." *Leadership and Policy in Schools* 16 (2): 328–56.

Cherryholmes, C. H. 1988. *Power and Criticism: Poststructural Investigations in Education*. Teachers College, Columbia University.

Deneen, P. J. 2008. "Strange Bedfellows: Allan Bloom and John Dewey Against Liberal Education, Rightly Understood." *Good Society Journal* 17 (2): 49–55.

Deneen, P. J. 2018. *Why Liberalism Failed.* Yale University Press.

Deng, Z. 2018. "Contemporary Curriculum Theorizing: Crisis and Resolution." *Journal of Curriculum Studies* 50 (6): 691–710.

Dewey, J. (1897) 2013. "My Pedagogic Creed." In *The Curriculum Studies Reader*, edited by D. J. Flinders and S. J. Thornton, 33–40. 4th ed. Routledge.

Dewey, J. (1910) 1933. *How We Think: A Restatement of the Relation of Reflective Thinking to the Educative Process.* 2nd ed. D.C. Heath (originally published by University of Michigan Press).

Dewey, J. 1916. *Democracy and Education.* Macmillan.

Dewey, J. (1929) 2007. *The Sources of a Science of Education.* Read Books (originally published by Horace Liveright).

Dewey, J. (1930) 1984. *Individualism Old and New.* Prometheus Books (originally published by University of California Press).

Dewey, J. (1934) 1962. *A Common Faith.* Yale University Press.

Dewey, J. 1938. *Logic: The Theory of Inquiry.* Henry Holt & Company.

Dewey, J. (1938) 1998. *Experience and Education: The 60th Anniversary Edition.* Kappa Delta Pi.

Dewey, J. (1939) 1989. *Freedom and Culture.* Prometheus (originally published by G.P. Putnam's Sons).

Dewey, J., and A. F. Bentley. 1949. *Knowing and the Known.* Beacon Press.

Dillon, J. T. 2009. "The Questions of Curriculum." *Journal of Curriculum Studies* 41 (3): 343–59.

Eisner, E. W. 1994a. *The Educational Imagination: On the Design and Evaluation of School Programs.* 3rd ed. Macmillan.

Eisner, E. W. 1994b. *Cognition and Curriculum Reconsidered.* 2nd ed. Teachers College Press.

Eisner, E. W. 2017. *The Enlightened Eye: Qualitative Inquiry and the Enhancement of Educational Practice.* 2nd ed. Teachers College Press.

Eisner, E. W., and E. Vallance. 1974. *Conflicting Conceptions of Curriculum. Series on Contemporary Educational Issues.* McCutchan.

English, A. R. 2013. *Discontinuity in Learning: Dewey, Herbart, and Education as Transformation.* Cambridge University Press.

Frankl, V. E. (1959) 2006. *Man's Search for Meaning.* Beacon Press.

Ferry, L. 1993. *Homo Aestheticus: The Invention of Taste in the Democratic Age.* Translated by R. De Loaiza. University of Chicago Press.

Freire, P. 1994. *Pedagogy of Hope: Reliving Pedagogy of the Oppressed.* Continuum.

Freire, P. 2018. *Pedagogy of the Oppressed.* Translated by Myra Bergman Ramos. Bloomsbury Academic.

Friesen, N., and H. Su. 2023. "What Is Pedagogy? Discovering the Hidden Pedagogical Dimension." *Educational Theory* 73 (1): 6–28.

Glasius, M. 2018. "What Authoritarianism Is . . . and Is Not : A Practice Perspective." *International Affairs* 94 (3): 515–33.

Glasius, M. et al. 2018. *Research, Ethics and Risk in the Authoritarian Field.* Palgrave Macmillan.

Good, J. A. 2006. *A Search for Unity in Diversity: The "Permanent Hegelian Deposit" in the Philosophy of John Dewey.* Rowman & Littlefield.

Goodwin, D. K. 2005. *Team of Rivals: The Political Genius of Abraham Lincoln.* Simon & Schuster.

Graue, M. E. 1993. *Ready for What? Constructing Meanings of Readiness for Kindergarten.* State University of New York Press.

Greene, M. 1988. *The Dialectic of Freedom.* Teachers College Press.

Hanh, T. N. (1975) 1987. *The Miracle of Mindfulness: An Introduction to the Practice of Meditation.* Beacon Press.

Havel, V. 1991. *Disturbing the Peace: A Conversation with Karel Hvížďala.* Translated by P. Wilson. Vintage.

Hegseth, P. 2022. *Battle for the American Mind: Uprooting a Century of Miseducation.* Broadside Books.

Henderson, J. G. 1980. *The Foreshadowing of Work and Play Elements in School Settings.* EdD dissertation, Stanford University.

Henderson, J. G. 1992. *Reflective Teaching: Becoming an Inquiring Educator.* Macmillan.

Henderson, J. G., and K. R. Kesson, eds. 1999. *Understanding Democratic Curriculum Leadership.* Teachers College Press.

Henderson, J. G. 2001. *Reflective Teaching: Professional Artistry Through Inquiry.* 3rd ed. Merrill/Prentice Hall.

Henderson, J. G. 2010. *The Path Less Taken: Immanent Critique in Curriculum and Pedagogy.* Edited by J. L. Schneider. Educator's International Press.

Henderson, J. G., ed. 2015. *Reconceptualizing Curriculum Development: Inspiring and Informing Action.* Routledge.

Henderson, J. G., D. J. Castner, and J. L. Schneider. 2018. *Democratic Curriculum Leadership: Critical Awareness to Pragmatic Artistry.* Rowman & Littlefield.

Henderson, J. G., and R. Gornik. 2007. *Transformative Curriculum Leadership.* 3rd ed. Merrill/Prentice Hall.

Henderson, J. G., and K. R. Kesson. 2004. *Curriculum Wisdom: Educational Decisions in Democratic Societies.* Merrill/Prentice Hall.

Hlebowitsh, P. S. 1990. "The Teacher Technician: Causes and Consequences." *Journal of Educational Thought/Revue de La Pensee Educative* 24 (3): 147–60.

Hlebowitsh, P. 2004. *Designing the School Curriculum.* Pearson/Allyn and Bacon.

Hlebowitsh, P. 2010. "Centripetal Thinking in Curriculum Studies." *Curriculum Inquiry* 40 (4): 503–13.

Hlebowitsh, P. 2021. "Ralph Tyler, the Tyler Rationale, and the Idea of Educational Evaluation." In *The Oxford Encyclopedia of Curriculum Studies*, edited by W. Schubert and M. F. He. Oxford University Press.

Hunter, J. H. 2024. *Democracy and Solidarity: On the Cultural Roots of America's Political Crisis.* Yale University Press.

Ingman, B. C., and C. M. Moroye. 2019. "Experience-Based Objectives." *Educational Studies: Journal of the American Educational Studies Association* 55 (3): 346–67.

Jefferson, T. 1786, August 13. "From Thomas Jefferson to George Wythe, 13 August 1786." Founders Online, National Archives. Accessed November 17, 2024. https://founders.archives.gov/documents/Jefferson/01-10-02-0162.

Joseph, P. B. 2011. *Cultures of Curriculum.* 2nd ed. Routledge.

Joseph, P. B. 2021. "Cultures of Curriculum." *Oxford Research Encyclopedia of Education.*

Jung, C. G. 1970. *Psychology and Religion: West and East. Collected Works of C. G. Jung.* Vol. 11. Princeton University Press.

Kelly, T. 1989. "Leading Class Discussions of Controversial Issues." *Social Education* 53 (6): 368–70.

Kelly, T. 2004. "A Teacher Educator's Story." In *Curriculum Wisdom: Educational Decisions in Democratic Societies*, edited by J. G. Henderson and K. R. Kesson, 144–57. Pearson/Merrill Prentice Hall.

Kelly, T. 2010. "Engaging Dissensus: Selected Principles and Reflections." In *The Path Less Taken: Immanent Critique in Curriculum and Pedagogy*, edited by J. G. Henderson et al., 91–96. Educator's International Press.

Kelly, T. 2014. "Transcending False Dichotomies: Confronting One of Life's Consistently Compelling Challenges." In *Experiencing Dewey: Insights for Today's Classroom*, edited by D. A. Breault and R. Breault. 2nd ed., 95–98. Routledge.

Kliebard, H. M. 1970. "The Tyler Rationale." *Sch Rev* 78 (2): 259–72.

Kliebard, H. M. 2004. *The Struggle for the American Curriculum, 1893–1958.* RoutledgeFalmer.

Kuhn, T. S. 1962. *The Structure of Scientific Revolutions.* University of Chicago Press.

Macdonald, J. B. (1971) 2000. "Curriculum Theory." In *Curriculum Studies: The Reconceptualization*, edited by W. Pinar, 5–13. Educator's International Press (originally published in *Journal of Educational Research*).

Macdonald, J. B. (1974) 1995. *Theory as a Prayerful Act: The Collected Essays of James B. Macdonald.* Edited by B. J. Macdonald. Peter Lang Publishing.

MacDonald, J. B., and D. E. Purpel. 1987. "Curriculum and Planning: Visions and Metaphors." *Journal of Curriculum and Supervision* 2 (2): 178–92.

Markkula Center for Applied Ethics. 2021. "A Framework for Ethical Decision Making." Accessed November 2024. https://www.scu.edu/ethics/ethics-resources/a-framework-for-ethical-decision-making/.

McClintock, R. 1971. "Toward a Place for Study in a World of Instruction." *Teachers College Record* 73 (2): 161–205.

McConnell, C., B. Conrad, and B. P. Uhrmacher. 2020. *Lesson Planning with Purpose: Five Approaches to Curriculum Design.* Teachers College Press

McKeon, R. 1952. "Philosophy and Action." *Ethics* 62 (2): 79–100.

Meyer, A., D. H. Rose, and D. Gordon. 2014. *Universal Design for Learning: Theory and Practice.* CAST Professional Publishing.

Michael-Luna, S.C., and D. Castner. 2023. "Removing the Guardrails of Democracy: Silencing Critique of Early Childhood Policy and Practice." *Contemporary Issues in Early Childhood* 24 (4):500–506.

Michael-Luna, S.C., and D. Castner. 2024. "Rising Authoritarian Practice in Early Childhood Curriculum: A Case Study" *Culture Studies & Critical Methodologies* 25(1).

Moroye, C. M., and P. B. Uhrmacher. 2009. "Aesthetic Themes of Education." *Curriculum & Teaching Dialogue* 11 (1–2): 85–101.

Muller, J., and M. Young. 2019. "Knowledge, Power and Powerful Knowledge Re-Visited." *Curriculum Journal* 30 (2): 196–214.

National Commission on Excellence in Education. 1983. *A Nation at Risk: The Imperative for Educational Reform*. D. P. Gardner, chair. US Department of Education.

Newmann, F. M., and D. W. Oliver. 1970. *Clarifying Public Controversy: An Approach to Teaching Social Studies*. Little, Brown & Co.

Nieman, S. 2023. *Left Is Not Woke*. Polity Press.

Noddings, N. 1984. *Caring: A Feminine Approach to Ethics and Moral Education*. University of California Press.

Noddings, N. 1992. Foreword. In J. G. Henderson, *Reflective Teaching: Becoming an Inquiring Educator*. Macmillan.

Noddings, N. 2001. "Care and Coercion in School Reform." *Journal of Educational Change* 2 (1): 35–43.

Noddings, N. 2013. *Education and Democracy in the 21st Century*. Teachers College Press.

Null, W. 2017. *Curriculum: From Theory to Practice*. 2nd ed. Rowman & Littlefield.

Null, W. 2023. *Curriculum: From Theory to Practice*. 3rd ed. Rowman & Littlefield.

Nussbaum, M. C. 2011. *Creating Capabilities: The Human Development Approach*. The Belknap Press.

Pinar, W. F. 1999. Foreword. In *Understanding Democratic Curriculum Leadership*, edited by J. G. Henderson and K. R. Kesson, x–xvi. Teachers College Press.

Pinar, W. F. 2006. *The Synoptic Text Today and Other Essays: Curriculum Development after the Reconceptualization*. Peter Lang Publishing.

Pinar, W. F. 2007. *Intellectual Advancement Through Disciplinarity: Verticality and Horizontality in Curriculum Studies*. Sense Publishers.

Pinar, W. F. 2013. *Curriculum Studies in the United States: Present Circumstances, Intellectual Histories*. Palgrave Macmillan.

Pinar, W. F., W. M. Reynolds, P. Slattery, and P. M. Taubman. 1995. *Understanding Curriculum: An Introduction to the Study of Historical and Contemporary Curriculum Discourses*. Peter Lang Publishing.

Postman, N. 1979. "Propaganda." *ETC: A Review of General Semantics* 36 (2): 128–33. http://www.jstor.org/stable/42575397.

Postman, N. 1988. "The Educationist as Painkiller." *English Education* 20 (1): 7–17. http://www.jstor.org/stable/40172665.

Reid, W. A. 1999. *Curriculum as Institution and Practice: Essays in the Deliberative Tradition*. Lawrence Erlbaum Associates.

Ryan, F. X. 2011. *Seeing Together: Mind, Matter and the Experimental Outlook of John Dewey and Arthur F. Bentley*. The American Institute for Economic Research.

Sahlberg, P. 2011. *Finnish Lessons: What Can the World Learn from Educational Change in Finland?* Teachers College Press.

Sahlberg, P. 2015. *Finnish Lessons 2.0: What Can the World Learn from Educational Change in Finland?* Teachers College Press.

Schneider, J. L. 2010. "Situating the Editors' Introductions." In *The Path Less Taken: Immanent Critique in Curriculum and Pedagogy*, edited by J. G. Henderson et al., 15–17. Educator's International Press.

Schneider, J. L. 2015. "Introducing Lead-Learning Stories: A Narrative Montage." In *Reconceptualizing Curriculum Development: Inspiring and Informing Action*, edited by J. G. Henderson et al., 140–43. Routledge.

Schwab, J. J. 1983. "The Practical 4: Something for Curriculum Professors to Do." *Curriculum Inquiry* 13 (3): 239–65.

Schwab, J. J. 2013. "The Practical: A Language for Curriculum." *Journal of Curriculum Studies* 45 (5): 591–621.

Stanley, J. 2024. *Erasing History: How Fascists Rewrite the Past to Control the Future*. One Signal Publishers/Atria.

Stanley, M. 1983. "The Mystery of the Commons: On the Indispensability of Civic Rhetoric." *Social Research* 50 (4).

Tanner, D., and L. Tanner. 2007. *Curriculum Development: Theory into Practice*. Pearson Merrill/Prentice Hall.

Tienken, C. 2017. *Defying Standardization: Creating Curriculum for an Uncertain Future*. Rowman & Littlefield.

Tulku, T. (1978) 1990. *Openness Mind: Self-Knowing and Inner Peace Through Meditation*. Dharma Publishing.

Tyler, R. W. 1949. *Basic Principles of Curriculum and Instruction*. University of Chicago Press.

Vallance, E. 1986. "A Second Look at Conflicting Conceptions of Curriculum." *Theory into Practice* 25 (1): 24. https://doi-org.proxyiub.uits.iu.e du/10.1080/00405848609543194.

Walker, A. 1982. *The Color Purple*. Simon & Schuster.

Walker, D. F. 1971, November. "The Process of Curriculum Development: A Naturalistic Model." *School Review* 80: 51–65.

Walker, D. 2003. *Fundamentals of Curriculum: Passion and Professionalism*. Lawrence Erlbaum Associates.

Walker, D. F. 2022. *Curriculum Deliberation*. Routledge. https://doi. org/10.4324/9781138609877-REE42-1.

Walker, D. F., and J. F. Soltis. 2009. *Curriculum and Aims*. 5th ed. Teachers College Press.

Wang, H. 2024. *Awakening to the Calling of Nonviolence in Curriculum Studies*. Peter Lang Publishing.

Webster, N. 1831. *The American Spelling Book*. George Goodwin & Sons.

Wiggins, G., and J. McTighe 2005. *Understanding by Design*. 2nd ed. Association for Supervision and Curriculum Development.

Wilentz, S. 2005. *The Rise of American Democracy: Jefferson to Lincoln*. W. W. Norton & Company.

Zhao, Y. 2018. *What Works May Hurt: Side Effects in Education*. Teachers College Press.